Europe On My Toes

A Ballet Dancer's Diary

Contents

Dedication

To all dancers, everywhere.

Introduction

Have you ever wondered what becomes of the little girls who dream of becoming a ballet dancer, get a professional job, do well in their job, but never actually make it to the top of their profession? Darcey Bussell is a household name these days, but what happens to the multitudes who do not become a Darcey Bussell?

To be at the top of the Ballet profession, it takes a body of steel with endless stamina, a mind of iron with relentless determination, a soul of depth with individual artistic expression, and the ability to take direction with humility. It also takes a lot of good fortune: to be in the right place at the right time, be ready to grasp an opportunity, and to stay fit and healthy and not be prey to injury.

This is my story, the story of a little girl who dreamed of becoming a ballerina. A very determined little girl, with some talent, a lot of artistry, but "physical limitations" - a description of her body's capabilities which plagued her career. How did that determined little girl get a job as a dancer? How far did she get in her dream to reach the top?

This book is taken directly from diaries and letters. Some names have been changed to respect the privacy of those people. The writing style is immature in the early years which reflects the age and experience when it was written, and it matures with time. It is direct and honest. It is a real story. I invite you to share my adventures as a professional dancer from 1976 to 1986 based in four different European countries.

Ysabelle Taylor 2019

Chapter One

Early Days

It was my mother's idea to send me to dance classes. She had enjoyed Greek dancing and roller skating as a hobby when she was younger. My main problem was not a dislike of dancing, but a fear of the other children. As an only child I was embarrassingly shy, hiding under my mother's skirt when introduced to strangers. I was well into adulthood before I learned to overcome this shyness.

One of the outstanding memories of my childhood is the annual holiday in Switzerland and Holland where we visited my mother's relatives. We spent the most time in Switzerland, often six or seven weeks in the summer. La Tour de Peilz on the Lake of Geneva came to be like a second home to me. I spent many a happy hour basking in the sun, sitting on the edge of the lake, watching the light change on the panorama of mountains opposite. It was here that I took my first independent steps to walk. It was also from here that I flew off to take up my first professional contract.

I was a very creative child, always able to entertain myself and was accustomed to being alone. I would make things out of anything I could find: yogurt cups, foil, paper, cardboard. I also wrote poems and painted pictures. The creative energy was gradually channeled into the dancing which became my greatest joy. Later, as a professional struggling to maintain the physical condition necessary for constant performance, I asked myself why I didn't become a painter or poet instead. Dancing is such a gruelling profession and I had no athletic inclinations, which certainly would have helped. I came to the conclusion that it was a mixture of the inspiration of music, and the creative spirituality and sensuality of movement in dance, which attracted me.

Showing potential to excel academically, I did well at school, winning a scholarship to a local private school in South East London when I was eleven. I did not achieve as much as I might have because I spent too much time day dreaming about dancing, and my basic laziness encouraged me to do the minimum work necessary to get by. Besides I was more interested in reading about the history of ballet and teaching myself Russian (because of the importance of Russian training in ballet development), than in any of my school subjects. The covers of my school books were adorned with doodles of ballet dancers.

I was often depressed and moody as a teenager. My father worked most evenings as well as during the days, and consequently I saw very little of him. My mother supervised me most of the time. I felt lonely and isolated. She probably did too. Our relationship was fraught. Ballet was my escape.

My dream was to study at the Royal Ballet School in London. I knew it offered the best ballet training in England which would be a passport to employment afterwards. I was dissuaded from auditioning when I was eleven. Apart from the fact that I was quite fat and would surely not have been accepted, my father insisted I complete a full time academic education until I was sixteen. Later I came to appreciate the value of this.

My frustration at not attending a full time Ballet school, and only having a few classes in the evenings and on Saturdays, propelled me to practise regularly at home and educate myself in the rich tradition of Russian Ballet, Diaghilev and the founding of British Ballet. I satisfied my appetite for classical music and art galleries and developed a dedication, commitment and belief that I was destined to dance.

I must have been about twelve when my father invited a talented young cellist, whose recital had greatly impressed him, to our home. My father joked about him being an Eskimo because his name was Thomas Igloi, but in fact he was Hungarian. Tom's family had fled to England during the 1956 uprising. He was a charming man with tremendous warmth of spirit and, as his visits became more frequent and we regularly attended his concerts, I became aware of a strong feeling of fondness toward him. Over the years this grew into an obsessive passion, though my feelings were never made known to Tom. After all, he was eleven years my senior. I expected to have to wait until I was well into adulthood before he would even consider reciprocating my sentiments.

Through my teenage years my preoccupation with romantic daydreams about this exceptionally gifted musician almost exceeded my involvement with ballet. I worked hard at school so I would make a better wife for Tom rather than a better dancer. One of the most rewarding and exciting experiences was when Tom came to watch me dance a solo at a prize winners' concert of a local ballet competition. At fourteen I had won two challenge cups. But for me the real prize was to perform knowing that Tom was in the audience. I shall never forget the look he gave me after the show when he came with my parents to meet me backstage, as if he was seeing me for the first time. After that I found it easier to talk with him and he took an interest in my dancing.

At last when I was fifteen I was able to audition for the Royal Ballet School in Barons Court. I passed the preliminary auditions and then applied for a scholarship. This was awarded to a boy, but as runner up, I was offered a place at the school subject to passing an orthopaedic examination. The fact that I failed to pass it should have been a warning to me. The school took me on anyway on the strength of my artistic qualities for a one year trial. It was the Easter holidays. The summer term was one of the happiest times of my life. With surprising maturity I realised that I had everything to hope for and nothing to regret.

Once I came to terms with having achieved my dream of many years, I had to set new challenges for myself and I worked with ambition to be successful. Like most of the students I dreamed of working with the Royal Ballet Company. At the school I had to deal with my first real disappointments. Though I worked very hard, I had physical problems of which I had been blissfully unaware until now. A stiff lower spine and tilted pelvis made it very difficult for me to acquire a strong, virtuosic ballet technique. Also, my shape was feminine and curvy, not straight and thin as was the fashion. Consequently, I felt rejected when girls less industrious than I, but with better physiques and techniques than mine, were promoted to higher classes or taken into the company. It took ten years for me to realise that by not getting into the Royal Ballet, many more interesting and varied opportunities were to be mine.

The physical struggle was tough. I was constantly tired, often had colds and doubtless made matters worse by erratic eating habits as I tried to slim to the desired stick shape. I watched friends blow up like balloons, and others become anorexic. All ballet dancers are concerned with body size and shape. Some are able to control it; some are not. I felt helplessly out of control, but somehow managed to become neither obese, nor skinny.

I had performed many times in dancing school shows, but as a student at the Royal Ballet School I had the chance to dance at the Royal Opera House in Covent Garden and these performances were the highlight of my student life.

My first performance was a walk on part in a gala in March 1975. I was a nun in a funeral procession in the *Don Juan* pas de deux by the choreographer John Neumeier danced by Margot Fonteyn and Rudolf Nureyev. I considered it to be an auspicious debut.

****

11

March 3rd 1975

I have now had two stage rehearsals at Covent Garden. The big night is tomorrow. It is, needless to say, thrilling for me to be backstage and onstage at the Opera House. It is like a maze of corridors and dressing rooms, and there are so many stairs …. The stage itself seems much smaller when you stand on it than it appears from a distance in the audience.

Standing in the wings I have seen the whole of the *Don Juan* pas de deux in rehearsal. Fonteyn and Nureyev dance superbly together. I am struck by her power of concentration and ruthless determination. Nureyev often mutters to her stopping the music when something goes wrong. Fonteyn however continues regardless, entirely immersed in her work.

The excitement of the past few days has been quite overwhelming. The auditorium looks rather as I imagined it would from the stage, but I'm sure I'll be terrified when there are thousands of people sitting in the seats watching.

****

That summer I performed the role of a neighbour - sometimes called the boy's mother - in the Royal Ballet School performance of Frederick Ashton's *The Two Pigeons* at the Big Top Tent in Battersea Park with Nicola Katrak and Stephen Beagley in the principal roles. I had originally been chosen to audition for the part of the principal gypsy girl, but my lack of technical proficiency, and also my lack of confidence in the dancing with the boys in pas de deux, lost me the opportunity. I ended up with a mime role, and as the youngest performer played the oldest character. I was however thrilled to be onstage involved in the production, and appreciated that I had been entrusted with some responsibility. I found it difficult to involve myself in a character part with no steps to dance and the drama teacher was asked to give me some special coaching. Eventually I discovered a way of thinking myself into my character's thoughts, so I really became the old woman whilst onstage, even whispering to the other performers in character.

I remained faithfully in love with Tom. He was close to my parents and we saw him often. My heart would miss a beat and my knees would tremble every time. Perhaps my obsession was a way of avoiding meeting young men nearer my own age and going out with them. I always refused invitations to parties or discos. Nonetheless, my feelings were precious and all important to me. Gradually I emerged from my cocoon of shyness and communication with Tom became easier. I started to be able to initiate conversations in a relaxed manner and saw a tangible possibility of our being friends eventually.

During my second year (to my relief I passed the one year trial), I felt more secure with the familiarity of the school, but began to be aware that I must consider auditioning for a job. I had always hoped to dance in England, but practicality suggested I look at the possibilities further afield. The Dutch National Ballet in Amsterdam had a good reputation and I had relatives in Holland so this seemed a sensible choice.

****

January 17th 1976

So here I am in Holland and the battle is just beginning. There were about fifty girls and ten boys at the audition. Rudi van Dantzig (director of the Dutch National Ballet) explained at the beginning that as there were so many of us, he would have to ask some of us to leave. He asked two to go before we even started. Then he walked along the rows of dancers at the barre weeding people out. It was at the end of the battements frappés exercise when he came up to me, shook his head and said "No". That was it and off I went.

Words cannot really describe how I felt. I was hot and flustered. My world had collapsed around me with one word and I felt deeply humiliated. I resolved to question him when the audition was over. I had not come all the way from London for twenty minutes of barre work to go away not knowing what was wrong with me.

I waited two hours in the theatre canteen and finally was able to see him. When I asked why he had sent me out, he could not remember. I told him outright that I did not think he had given me a fair chance to be seen. Where did I get the courage? He was very polite and suggested I do class on Monday when he will try to come and look at me.

January 18th 1976

I was taken by a Dutch cousin to Scapino Ballet's *Nutcracker* today. I liked the production and thought it ambitious for a company of only twenty-eight dancers to attempt a full length classical ballet. There were many young, enthusiastic dancers in the group.

Afterwards we went backstage and I asked to see the director, something I would never have dared to do before this weekend. We found a very nice ballet mistress who told me that there are no vacancies this year. I gave her a photograph with my name and address and she suggested I try next year. She really put me at ease.

13

I feel that I have grown up and changed in these last few days. I have done things I would never have dreamed of doing before; and having done them once, it will not be so hard another time. Now however, I have tomorrow to live up to, and that makes me nervous of course. But I shall not be meek; I believe in myself and I shall do all in my power to make them believe in me too!

January 19th 1976

Last night I tossed and turned for hours worrying about how on earth I'd had the nerve to confront Rudi van Dantzig, and how I was going to cope today.

At ten o'clock this morning I was ready to do class at the theatre but was told to wait till eleven fifteen when there was an audition. So I waited....

There were six boys and eight other girls auditioning, all of whom seemed years older than me. As soon as he saw me in leotard and tights Rudi van Dantzig told me I had been sent out because my hips and bottom are too big. That did not surprise me, but my heart sank. Anyway, I was determined to get a free class if nothing else; besides I had not lost yet, he had not seen me dance.

Whilst dancing I didn't feel too bad, but between exercises I felt nauseous. I was dripping with sweat, dry with thirst and I just could not stop the nerves. However, I kept going and little by little gained the attention of the people watching. I think they were amused to see what I could produce.

I was surprised when we were all allowed into the centre after the barre work, and later there was pointe work for the girls. Three girls were then asked to stay behind to do fouettés and to my utter amazement I was one of them. The first girl started with a double turn followed by thirty two faultless fouettés. The second did three singles and a double up to thirty two. I was almost embarrassed to present thirty two single turn fouettés, but they seemed impressed that at seventeen I could accomplish this technical feat.

An interview with Rudi van Dantzig followed. I could not believe it when I was standing in the same place as Saturday outside his office, only this time he had asked to see me! He told me I sickle my feet (curving the ankle line), my muscles don't show and I must lose weight. There might be a place for me in the company but he wants to see me again. So I'll stay a few more days to do classes.

January 21st 1976

Two classes are over and I am none the wiser. Rudi van Dantzig watched yesterday, not today, which is just as well since I've been feeling sick - due to nerves probably. He told me he did not know if there is a place yet, but if there is one, he will write to me so I can come and do classes and he can see if I've lost weight.

I can't say I'm disappointed because I couldn't really have hoped for more. There is still a chance. This visit to Holland has been very worthwhile. I have learnt so much and done so many new things.

****

I never heard from the Dutch National Ballet, but in the spring I returned to Amsterdam to do classes again. I saw Rudi van Dantzig but he told me I was still too fat. Somehow my desperate desire to lose weight had made it impossible for me to do so.

Easter 1976 was memorable in the devastation of events on my family's life. My father had been gradually suffering from increased back trouble, probably caused by war injuries. He had been a glider pilot during the Second World War. Now he was relying heavily on pain killers and missing many days from work. I was unaware of the severity of the situation as I was so absorbed by own problems of growing up and finding a job. I was to be jolted out of my self indulgent thoughts however, to re-evaluate the meaning of life.

****

April 17th 1976

This evening I was in the kitchen making supper. I heard my mother scream and then my father came in. He was crying. My wonderful, big, strong father was crying … I've never seen him cry. I knew someone had died and I tried to prepare myself for the shock. He sat down, put me on his lap, turned my head away from him and stroked my hair nervously. Then he told me that Tom had died during the night. Apparently he had a headache when he went to bed and never woke up. The only good thing is that he didn't suffer. My mother is almost as heartbroken as if I had died.

As for me, it just hasn't sunk in. It's made me feel very old and wise very suddenly. I've always tried to value life, but now I value it even more and appreciate the wisdom of a lady who wrote to a radio programme to tell them the best thing that had happened to her on Friday 13th. It was a competition. She said that the most wonderful thing that

15

happened to her was that she woke up. It has taught me yet again that, there is only one security in life and that is the present moment. One must appreciate each day, each hour, each minute, each second of one's life for what it is worth because life is ever changing and nothing is certain from one moment to the next; except that eventually we shall all die.

****

Tom's death made me feel horribly cheated by fate. Now I would never have the chance to get to know him properly. There were so many questions I wanted to ask him, and things I wanted to tell him.

During my second, final, year at the Royal Ballet School, I appeared in many performances of Verdi's opera *Rigoletto* with the Royal Opera at Covent Garden and was proud to be paid a student's wage for this work. The school performance that year was *Coppélia* at Covent Garden. Susan Lucas and Stephen Sheriff took the leads with David Bintley as Dr Coppelius. I enjoyed my parts as a soloist in the national dances in Act One, and "Work Hours" in Act Three, overcoming my shyness with the male students who partnered me.

I attended a few auditions in London for various companies but did not succeed in getting a job. When I left the Royal Ballet School in the summer of 1976 I was unemployed.

Chapter Two

Düsseldorf 1976 - 1979

After finishing my training, I planned to go on holiday to Switzerland with my parents. I attended open classes in London before we left. It was here that I met my friend Liz whom I had known for some years. We had seen little of each other the previous two years and were glad to meet again and catch up on each other's news. Liz had a contract to start work in Düsseldorf in West Germany in August. Naturally, I was envious and she nonchalantly suggested I go with her when she started work. She seemed convinced that another girl, who had been given a contract at the same time as her, was going to break it. "You'll be there instead!" She blissfully assured me. "They'll see you can put one foot in front of the other and give you her contract!" I told her she was mad - but I went. My mother agreed to buy me a return flight from Geneva to Düsseldorf.

It was extraordinary leaving home to go on holiday that summer. I knew I was going to audition in Germany, and deep inside me I knew I was leaving home, however unlikely the possibility of a contract seemed.

****

August 24th 1976

Here I am in Düsseldorf! My flight was superb. It was beautiful flying over the clouds and I was not frightened at all, as I thought I might be. When I arrived at the hotel I found Liz waiting for me.

Düsseldorf is a lovely city. It is rich and full of expensive boutiques. It's fun to go window shopping. Many of the streets are lined with trees and there are countless little cafes and restaurants to try. Every second shop is a chocolate or cake shop. Liz can't believe how good I am being about resisting temptation.

I have met the secretary of the Ballet company who told me to do classes this week. Erich Walter (the director) will see me when he is back next week. Rumour suggests that there is indeed a vacancy.

September 21st 1976

Isn't life strange? Just when everything seemed so bleak and grey, I woke up to find myself a member of the Düsseldorf Ballet (Ballett Der Deustche Oper Am Rhein to be precise); that distant German company I have heard of where the dancers get fantastic pay! It seems so pointless that I had to experience all those depressions and disappointments when this was waiting for me at the end of it all.

The classes are good and the studios have to be seen to be believed, they are so luxurious. The Royal Ballet in London would be envious. It is a shock to suddenly be paid such ridiculously high wages for doing the thing I love most. Again the dancers at home would envy me. I spend a third of my money renting a lovely little apartment in the centre of the city. I have a large bed-sitting room, a little hallway, kitchen and bathroom with a divinely large bathtub, and even a small balcony.

Leaving home to go and live alone in a foreign city is a large step to take, but I feel relatively secure as I have my work and speak some German. I feel more stable emotionally and have even lost three kilos in weight. I got a refund on the return ticket to Geneva and my parents visited on their way back to England helping me to find my flat and settle in.

September 24th 1976

Yesterday Erich Walter came to watch class and afterwards a cast list for fairies and cavaliers in *Sleeping Beauty* went up on the notice board. Guess what…! Yours truly is a second cast fairy, variation and all! I do the second solo, but Walter's version is completely different from the one I learned at school. The Entrée with six couples is long and complicated including lifts onto the boys' shoulders, promenades and pirouettes. Luckily the men are willing to practise the difficult parts with the women. Although it is difficult, I am not intimidated by it. This has boosted my confidence even though some of my friends are jealous.

When I am working, my work is all important and nothing can distract me. However, when I am not working I feel a little lost. I think of home, my friends and family, and I long for letters. I hate cooking for myself and have to fight the temptation to pop out for a hamburger or apple strudel. But every time I am tired and things seem grey I just think back to how I felt a month or two ago, and I am so thankful and relieved.

My work is going well. Sometimes I feel on top of my technique, sometimes I don't - but every day I work hard and enjoy it. My thigh work and jumps are still weak I know, but I feel stronger generally, and more confident. Épaulement and the use of the upper body are lacking in the other dancers here and I am trying to keep mine up because I think it is very important.

September 25th 1976

This evening brought my debut as a professional dancer. I got myself very worked up about it all because I had not been onstage for three months, but I felt comfortable once I was performing. There was an awkward moment when lights started flashing everywhere. No-one had warned me about that. Suddenly everything felt as if moving in slow motion. I was a lamenting woman in Walter's *Legend of Joseph* with music by Richard Strauss, but I've no idea what I was lamenting about! They misspelled my name in programme, so I'll have to complain about that.

I was disappointed to see we only give six performances in October and I will not necessarily be in all of them. Perhaps there will be more performances later, but this discovery led me to think that this might not be such a good company in which to work my way up. I have been thinking a lot recently about my chances of becoming a soloist with this company in a few years. I have come to the conclusion that the important thing is that I expand myself. I feel like a rubber balloon that must be blown up in order to bring out my true qualities. I shall leave when I feel the expanding slowing down. There is no doubt I am growing. I'm learning and working on many different ballets. I'm living away from home, improving my German, and I'm exploring Düsseldorf.

September 26th 1976

I was lying in bed on the point of dropping off to sleep when I thought I saw a flashing light and thought to myself "ah, someone has switched the light on in the hall". Then I woke up and realised that I'd been dreaming that I was at home in London. The bed was comfortable like my bed, the blanket was warm and soft like my blanket, and I heard traffic noise outside like in London. Now I feel wide awake and slightly shaky. Deep down inside I'm not really here; I'm still at home. It's an awful torn sort of feeling because most of my conscious self is here, but a part of me still has to work very hard at adapting. In many ways I feel disorientated.

It worries me that life can seem so bleak, when in truth I've never had so much going for me. I think I miss my friends: it takes time to make real friends.

I know it's silly to worry about such trivial things when my work is all that counts, but sometimes I worry because I've never had a boyfriend and I am so innocent about these things. I don't know the first thing about how to catch a man - besides I don't really want to. I would love so much

19

to have someone to take me out, to laugh with, have fun with and make me feel feminine and wanted. And yet even if someone turned up who could give me all these things, I wouldn't have the time or energy to appreciate them. I must not be distracted from my work. I'm wasting time indulging in self pity in my solitude. I always get these feelings of depression and female inadequacy before my period. Why do I have to be a woman? Why can't I be a man?

My weight is a sore subject. I think fluid retention is due to that wretched female curse. But it's miserable to be trying to lose weight and to watch the scales creeping up. I'm torn between not eating to slim and eating to keep up my strength. I feel so very young and fresh and inexperienced. In a way it's nice; in a way it's lonely.

October 12th 1976

My second performance in Germany saw me rushing around in the Sabbath at the end of Walter's *Symphonie Fantastique* to music by Berlioz. Falco Kapuste and Monique Janotta shone in the leading roles. She is a beautiful ballerina and inspires me enormously. I was masked again - hopefully no-one recognised me as all went fine until, as we ran off at the end, I made a great leaping exit and fell flat on my face!

This week we are travelling about thirty kilometres to Duisburg every day to rehearse for the premiere of Walter's *The Stone Flower* to music by Prokofiev. They did it in Düsseldorf last year. The new people have to learn everything in case someone falls sick or injures themselves. I find this frustrating because we do not get class in the morning and there is very little space backstage to work. I float about in the wings using bits of scenery as a barre and try to do exercises. It's difficult to keep concentrated with stage hands and dancers rushing past all the time. Most of all I'm desperate to be dancing on the stage instead of in the wings. I'm thankful not to be in a touring company. I'd find it very hard to maintain my technique in these circumstances.

October 30th 1976

The last rehearsal for *Giselle* was this afternoon and now the performance is unbelievably close. I cannot help being rather het up and I am coming out in nervous rashes. It is hard to remember all the steps and sequences and interpret them artistically when we have had so few rehearsals. We are rehearsing so many different ballets all the time. I want to make up the life (and death) story of my wili. I want to know who I was, why I am a wili now and why I hate men so much to want to drive Hilarion and Albrecht to their deaths. I want to feel that I have a woman's

20

soul captured in a spirit's presence. Then there is the courtier in Act One, another young lady I have to acquaint myself with.

Through all this I find myself thinking about the Dutch National Ballet. I think the reason I am so keen to go to Holland is because I have some roots there. The lack of them here isolates me. Sometimes I feel so terribly lonely. Although I think I fit into the company alright, I do not really belong here in this town, in this country. At least I have some security with Düsseldorf as a stable base and a regular salary. My privacy in my flat is important to me too.

I am frightened about *Giselle*. It is the most dancing I have ever done onstage in one performance. Some parts are technically difficult for me in this production and I get very breathless. I happen to be the wili who does a series of turns going from centre stage downstage straight towards the audience in the middle. Needless to say I'm frightened of coming off pointe, forgetting something and making such a terrible mess that everyone notices, or even of falling over completely. We have not had a stage rehearsal, or costume rehearsal, or even heard the orchestra playing the music.

November 2nd 1976

Yesterday I arrived three and a half hours early to prepare for the performance. I was very touched to receive telegrams from my parents and my first dancing teacher wishing me good luck. Small gifts and cards were exchanged and the atmosphere was charged with excitement.

My hair was done for me by the hairdressers as in all German theatres. I did not like the way they did it and thought we should have low classical buns rather than high ones. Anyhow it felt secure with dozens of pins in it.

I enjoyed the first act more than the second. I had more acting in the former and hated all the standing in Act Two during the variations and pas de deux. My big toe joints were inflamed and painful and it was miserable having to just stand there holding a pose. The dancing was enjoyable and I received compliments from various members of the company which was encouraging.

Afterwards I went out to a bar and disco in the Old Town with a group of dancers. We had great fun and ended up in one chap's flat making tea and sandwiches. Peter Breuer had danced Albrecht. He is a regular guest artist here and was also in the group I went out with. He is very handsome and I've got quite a crush on him!

Classes are getting faster and I find this hard as the exercises do not warm the body up properly. The pace used to be slower and I preferred this as the muscles had more time to be tuned up.

November 7th 1976

I have started going to opera performances on my nights off. It is free entertainment for employees of the Opera House. Perhaps I shall educate myself in the process. I only managed to sit through two acts of Wagner's *Tristan and Isolde* last night, my bottom got too sore! I don't know the first thing about opera, but the singing seemed very good and the audience gave warm ovations. I enjoyed the costumes and lights which were excellent. Next week I am going to see *Rigoletto*. I look forward to that as I remember dancing in it at Covent Garden.

November 9th 1976

I've got a cold! I know it is because I started a crash diet two days ago when I got such a shock when I weighed myself. I was also shocked and upset by my partner's rude comments about my weight in a rehearsal. It's true I should be lighter, but he is weak.

It's disconcerting to find that I suddenly do not enjoy what I have spent my whole life aiming to do. That is how I feel about *Giselle* tonight. Maybe I am trying too hard and taking it all too seriously, but I have found little satisfaction in any of the performances so far. The joy of dancing is lost when I have to concentrate on so many different things; remembering the steps, keeping in line in the corps de ballet, trying to present myself artistically. I expect this first year is going to be hard. It is also difficult because performances are few and far between, so there is no continuity. There are about two performances a week and not always of the same production. I'm sure I'd get over my nerves if we did the same ballet every night for a week. I long to be a soloist and have the opportunity to express myself as an individual, and yet I know this work in the corps de ballet is an essential part of my development that must be endured. Is it really worth it? What is waiting for me at the end of it all?

November 14th 1976

I am having a hard time with the classes. They are too fast for me and I lose the placing of my hips. Nonetheless, I do think I have gained strength since I've been here, especially on pointe. Almost all the ballets are on pointe and we spend most of the day in our pointe shoes.

Peter Breuer is here again and inspiring secret, sensual fantasies. I hope he can't read my thoughts!

I am so looking forward to my mother's visit. The promise of her arrival helps me get through the miserable moments. I miss home terribly; just the simple luxury of having my own belongings I grew up with around me.

A girl was poked by a spear in the lamenting women section of *Legend of Joseph* this evening during the performance and had to be carried home. This is a frenzied part with veiled women in long dresses dashing around the stage trying to avoid the men who dance with spears. It seems ridiculous to have to concentrate more on not getting hurt than on the actual performance.

November 16th 1976

It's not surprising I spend a lot of thoughts wondering what it is like in other companies when everything is such a mess here. We work from 10am till 1.30pm and 5.30 - 8.30pm, but so much time gets wasted because people mess around and do not take their work seriously enough. We have started rehearsing *L'Orfeo* with music by Gluck and choreography by Walter, but we have not finished putting *Sleeping Beauty* together yet. There's a lack of continuity in rehearsals as well as performances. There are a lot of injuries and the Waltz of the Flowers has already been cut from sixteen to fourteen girls. The company does not seem big enough even with sixty dancers.

I suspect people get injured easily partly because the classes are too fast and partly because there is not a good working atmosphere. There are a lot of tensions and the joy of dancing seems totally forgotten. Perhaps the generous private health insurance scheme that most of us belong to also encourages complacency.

November 29th 1976

It was sad to see my mother off at the airport. I can hardly believe she was here; it all seems like a dream now. It was thrilling to perform knowing that she was in the audience watching me and she was very excited about it all. She helped me a lot with domestic things and improving my eating habits. Somehow, I have just got to lose weight, maintaining it is not enough. I did not dare tell her that a ballet mistress has mentioned that I should watch my weight. At 54 kilos I am thinner than I was a few weeks ago, but fatter than I was when I auditioned here. I am not too heavy for 169 centimetres, but I do not look right.

At least my love of dancing has returned with the performances of *Sleeping Beauty*. Tchaikovsky's music is a joy to move to and I particularly like the third act where I am a courtier in a golden silk and lace gown with an elegant silver-grey wig. All the dancing is on pointe and the group has a lot to do in the opening Polonaise and closing Mazurka dances. I hope I'll be given the chance to dance one of the fairy solos one day, but the corps work in this production is challenging and I'm grateful for that.

I enjoyed my part as a shadow in the underworld in *L'Orfeo* too and was again inspired by Monique Janotta's beautifully controlled dancing.

After much deliberation I took the plunge and bought myself a black and white television set. It will be company and will help my German as all foreign films and programmes are dubbed into German.

December 3rd 1976

Erich Walter watched class today and afterwards started choreographing a new ballet to be premiered in January with two other new pieces. To my utter thrill and delight I am in it. It is for six couples plus four soloists to music by Bela Bartok. Really everything is going fantastically well for me; the only grey cloud is my weight. I am convinced all my problems would be solved if only I could lose weight; but it is so difficult. Even when I am super strict with myself I can't ever see any difference. I feel so self conscious sometimes. I am sure the men stare at my hips and hope they will not have to lift me.

I am so silly! Sometimes I lie in bed waiting for sleep to envelop me and I wonder how long it will be before I have a physical relationship. I even worry if I shall remain a virgin for the rest of my life, or never be kissed. Physical love is a mystery to me and I am both curious about it, and shy of it.

December 14th 1976

Rehearsals for the new programme are progressing. The choreography is becoming more and more complicated as time passes - steps and more steps. I don't really understand what Walter wants. He performs some movements resembling a tap routine to me. Then the older dancers, who know his way, interpret this into some recognisable ballet moves. I just copy them and hope for the best. So far this method seems to have worked.

We all wonder how on earth he is going to finish it all on time. The first movement is finished, but that is only ten minutes of a thirty minute ballet. Some people complain he is unmusical. He seems to follow the rhythm rather than the melody. It's good brain work but can be frustrating when he changes the timing slightly at each rehearsal.

Another ballet mistress has ticked me off about my weight and weak tummy and buttock muscles which is upsetting because I try so hard and practise on my own all the time. She shouts a lot in rehearsals which upsets me as well and her attitude makes me feel very small. But I battle on determined to surprise them all.

January 1st 1977
1977 and I welcome in the New Year with my parents and relatives in Holland.

I had a dreadful cold over Christmas and was very thankful to have my parents staying with me to comfort me. On my return to rehearsals after a few days break I was again reprimanded for being too fat. The direction is panicking because the costumes for the new ballet are white unitards. I felt very shocked by the insulting way I was told off, especially as I have not put on weight over Christmas. Probably my muscles have relaxed as I was ill, and they looked flabby. To say I was upset at the threat of being taken out of the premiere is the understatement of the year, especially as I had been losing weight before Christmas and no-one seemed to have noticed.

My parents saw a performance of *Giselle* a few days later and assured me that I am beautiful and did not look big onstage. This did help to boost my depleted ego a little, as I trust them to tell me the truth and not be blinded by their affection for me.

January 9th 1977
Bartok's *Divertimento* is finally finished. The ending is weird: the music finishes with a bang and we just go on dancing into the wings.

Many people in the company have 'flu and colds. I am one of the victims. I am worried how I am going to keep up my strength for the premiere and keep slim now I am almost 51 kilos. My cold is streaming and I am exhausted, so I went to a doctor who prescribed medicines and wrote me off sick from work for the rest of the week, but I shall try to go back sooner. The last couple of days have been hell. I have been so worried about being sick, my weight and the premiere next week. I got myself into such a desperate state that I 'phoned home and my father is coming over. He is off work at the moment because of his back trouble.

January 21st 1977
What excitement at the premiere! I received cards, telegrams, champagne and chocolates! The performance went very well and I got through everything, though I was very nervous of course. It had helped having

three dress rehearsals. Erich Walter wished everyone good luck individually beforehand. He seemed very tense before, but happy afterwards.

It is a relief it's all over. I was reprimanded for taking time off and was lucky not to lose my part. They're still telling me to lose weight.

February 6th 1977

I have already broken the new diet I started a few days ago after being told off about my weight again. The trouble is, I lose control when I am tired; and I'm tired all the time. I am beginning to suspect one of the ballet mistresses who is always hounding me about my weight, of jealousy. She stopped dancing recently and is still quite young. I do not understand why she is so cruel, sometimes attacking me between curtain calls during performances. Her attitude implies that the unfortunate audience is doomed to watch some hideous, fat creature lumbering about. If I really believed that, I would not be onstage.

The good news is that we are learning *Swan Lake* and I am a swan in Acts Two and Four and a peasant in Act One. I have always wanted to be a swan. We are being worked very hard and everyone is complaining. I don't mind corrections but I do wish we would not be shouted at. I suppose it must be difficult to get a group of sixteen women to dance in unison, but I think people tend to rebel rather than cooperate when they are not treated with respect.

A lot of dancers are leaving this year which doesn't say much for the state of the company: six boys and seven girls, including my friend Liz. Unfortunately all the girls are short so there will not be many new opportunities for tall ones like myself. Height is very important in casting ballets. New dancers like me have to fit the costumes of the departed ones for one thing. There also needs to be a balance between the heights of the men and women in a group.

February 16th 1977

I am very tired and in desperate need of a rest. Part of the reason for this is that I often find myself offering overnight accommodation to dancers who come to audition for the company. I lose sleep looking after them, but I enjoy the company.

Classes tire and frustrate me. I am sure they are totally wrong for my body and the corrections I am given are wrong for me. I know they cause me to tense incorrect muscles in my buttocks and put my weight too far back on my heels. There is too much emphasis on doing movements forcefully which I'm sure is dangerous. A dancer's relationship with her teachers is so important. Without trust and respect it is impossible to progress. I am not the only one in the company to find fault with the classes but no-one does anything about changing things.

I also get frustrated because I want so much to "give" and enjoy my performances, but someone always comes along to ruin my happiness assuring me I was out of line, off the music, or looked fat. I know I should be resilient and learn to accept the criticism but it is given in such an insulting manner here.

There was the first performance of *Swan Lake* tonight but I was not able to find much pleasure in it. We only finished learning the first act a couple of days ago and had never run it through properly. There are three long dances for the corps de ballet in Act One and I thought I was going to die at the end I had such a bad stitch. After this I was ticked off about being out of line and warned to watch the lines in Act Two. Consequently all my concentration went into this and I felt unable to express anything artistically. I hate to be mechanical. By the end of the evening I was totally exhausted of course and then had great difficulty unwinding and getting to sleep.

My weight is going down and I am sneezing again.

February 18th 1977

Two things have cheered me up today. Firstly, I was complimented by one of the dancers on the quality of my dancing. To gain the respect of one's colleagues is most satisfying. Secondly, the subject of weight came up in the dressing room and I was surprised to discover that I am lighter than most of the girls who are my height.

February 24th 1977

It was Carnival time in Düsseldorf last weekend. Everyone seemed merry and festive and the streets were littered with confetti and streamers which were magically cleared by the following morning.

Liz and I wandered through the crowds of people and beer stalls watching a procession of floats. We were taking photographs and watching the people when I was suddenly grabbed from behind and kissed passionately on the lips. At the time I panicked and ran away as soon as I was able. According to Liz, as I didn't really see him, he was tall, dark and handsome, and definitely had a touch of Omar Sharif about him. I'm still kicking myself and I suspect Liz wished it had happened to her!

March 7th 1977

Every day I start a new diet, and every day I break that diet. Somehow I have to pull myself together. My period is due and I am suffering all the usual symptoms. I suspect that is one of the reasons for my uncontrollable tiredness right now. I'm going to try really hard tomorrow to diet and rest and keep myself cheerful. I seem quite cheerful most of the time, but then all of a sudden my tiredness will hit me and catch me unawares. My mind just seems so mixed up at the moment. I don't seem able to control my thoughts which seem constantly centred on the past and London. When I drift into those fantasies they seem more real than my life here in Düsseldorf which feels like a dream.

March 9th 1977

We have started rehearsing for the next premiere. The programme will include *La Bayadère* Act Two and *Les Sylphides*. I don't know how they expect to do the former with only sixteen girls instead of the usual thirty-two.

I offered my "hotel" services to two victims of the recently disbanded Ballet International Company who came to audition here. I am now very thankful not to have obtained a contract with that company when I auditioned last year. My visitors watched a performance and it was interesting to hear their comments. They think the standard of dancing here is high and that I am lucky to have my job.

I am counting the minutes till I fly home next week when we have a holiday.

March 14th 1977

It happened last night ….. the thing I have feared most since I have been here …..Erich Walter was very rude to me about my weight in front of the company. He was calmer later in private and suggested I get a diet from a doctor. I managed not to crumble in the studio but I burst into floods of tears afterwards. Others were picked on during the rehearsal, but the main outburst was at me; and it came very suddenly. I felt numb. People were kind and thought I had been badly treated. They tried to console me by reminding me that some directors prefer female dancers to have unfeminine shapes. The ideal for them is an almost masculine outline with as few curves as possible. Perhaps I should consider a cosmetic operation to remove some fat tissue from my buttocks - but there's no way I can alter the shape of my skeleton.

March 24th 1977

It was so, so wonderful to be at home again, in many ways as if I had never been away. I saw friends, attended performances and had some coaching from Janet Lewis, the teacher whose lessons had helped me to be accepted into the Royal Ballet School. The only black cloud was having to return to Düsseldorf.

I am still taking vitamin pills, diuretics, and appetite suppressants and have even started smoking small cigars in the attempt to avoid over eating. Nonetheless, they have threatened to take me out of *Divertimento* which we perform again in April if I am not thin. These people are very crafty at evading responsibility. It was one of the ballet mistresses who told me that another one, with more influence, would take me out if I do not lose weight.

We are rehearsing Vivaldi's *Four Seasons*. I am glad to be an understudy as there is a very tense atmosphere, especially when Erich Walter comes into the studio. No-one seems to enjoy their work here. Surely it is different elsewhere?

March 30th 1977

I am in *Sacre du Printemps* (Walter's choreography) which we are learning now for a double bill with the *Four Seasons*. I am glad to be in it, but am getting bruises and sore muscles from the floor work and contemporary movements which include a lot of contractions.

I feel very sleepy and depressed all the time and cry a lot. I tried to go to the doctor today but all the surgeries are shut on Wednesdays. That made me feel more wretched of course. I have been feeling so desperate and homesick since returning to Germany, and I am haunted by memories of Walter's outburst. I feel as if everything is turning against me. I can't see the future clearly.

April 1st 1977

Two days ago all I wanted in the whole world was to curl up and fall asleep in the security of my own bed at home for a long time. My wishes have been granted.

I went to see the doctor, tried to explain my problems and burst into tears. He diagnosed low blood pressure and wrote me off sick for two weeks. He prescribed medication for the blood pressure and tranquillisers. So I went and booked myself on a flight to London. I risk losing my parts in all the ballets, but I've just got to sort myself out.

April 23rd 1977

When I arrived back in Düsseldorf the sun was shining. Everything looked summery and continental; even the taxi driver was nice to me. It was a relief as I had left London feeling unsure after the break. My parents were marvellously supportive. I rested a lot at home and got back into shape with coaching from Janet Lewis. I got a sick note for another week from my English doctor.

Strangely people have commented that I look thinner, but I have not lost weight. I believe I look better because I am working better after the coaching sessions. By controlling the muscles in the lower spine, pelvis and thighs better, I am creating a slimmer image.

I found myself thrown into performances straight away as a lot of dancers are injured. I am glad I have my place in the new programme in *La Bayadère* Act Two and *Les Sylphides*. People have been very nice to me, concerned about my health. I am feeling positive about my weight problem and accept that I must deal with it positively and sensibly.

There is much discontent in the company and regular tears in the dressing rooms. Tranquillisers have been prescribed for others too. It is a pity there is always such a fraught atmosphere. It is no wonder the dancers tense their necks.

Good news is that I am finally dancing in the *The Stone Flower* replacing a sick girl.

May 30th 1977

I have been quite contented the past weeks with both my dancing and my social life as I have had visitors and made new friends in the company. There have been blue skies and the spring blossoms are beautiful.

Work has been full and hectic with preparations for the premiere. *La Bayadère* is nerve wracking as it is technically very demanding on all the dancers. The corps de ballet make the famous entrance of arabesques and back bends filing on down a ramp. Being tall, I am one of the last to enter so I have fewer arabesques to do than the first ones. The adagio section which follows is also terrifying. If one girl wobbles, it puts everyone off and it is disastrous if concentration is lost.

The corps de ballet was cheered after *Les Sylphides* giving worthy credit to Lynn Wallis who mounted it for us. It was lovely to work with her as she was one of my teachers at the Royal Ballet School. This ballet is easier technically than *La Bayadère*, but posing during the variations requires great discipline. It is at such times when I am poised onstage in a group of elegant sylphs that I have to resist the urge to scratch my nose!

June 28th 1977

My mother came to stay with me during the week of my 19th birthday and now a friend is visiting for the last two weeks of the season. But the real thrill at the moment is that in six days I shall dance the second fairy in *Sleeping Beauty* replacing an injured girl. I am both delighted and terrified, and practise the part on my own everyday in addition to my rehearsals.

July 4th 1977

Tonight was very special and a milestone in my career. I have been terribly nervous all week and was petrified before the performance. Somehow, I managed to remain calm when I was dancing. The solo went well. I wish I could have more rehearsals and performances to work on it now. The orchestra played a steady speed which helped my dancing and there seemed to be a good spontaneous applause. I had tears running down my cheeks as I ran offstage into the wings. The rest of the performance was an ordeal to get through as I had poured all my energy into the solo.

I received many compliments from members of the company and even from the ballet mistress. But the most satisfying one came from the stage manager who told me he had enjoyed watching me.

It has been a tough year for me in many ways, but I feel very optimistic about the experience I have gained, especially having danced my first professional solo. Now I am looking forward to spending my well deserved holiday with my parents in Switzerland.

****

September 20th 1977

It wasn't easy coming back to Düsseldorf, but I am feeling more settled now. I'm happy to be cast as a fairy in *Sleeping Beauty*. Unfortunately, there are only a few performances and insufficient rehearsals, so I shall have to practise on my own a lot. However, it's exciting to see my name up on the posters around town as a soloist in this production.

There are new parts for me in other productions in the corps de ballet and I am enjoying performances more this year. My weight is reasonable at around 51 kilos, with the occasional help of diuretics and appetite suppressants. However, I don't feel secure about it at all and wish I was thinner.

October 31st 1977

I have had visits from my parents who came separately so I would have company for longer. My mother was able to see me dance my solo in *Sleeping Beauty* which was nice for both of us. I had a bad cold during my father's visit which reduced my capacity for enjoying it. His back is still bad and he is talking seriously about taking early retirement.

31

Walter's *Romeo and Juliet* is a big disappointment. It has such wonderful music by Prokofiev and I have strong memories of Kenneth MacMillan's production in London. It is sad to find myself involved in a drab and uninspired version.

I am cover for the other programme we are currently rehearsing. I don't understand why I am not in it. Are they angry with me? Or are they giving me a rest? Anyway, I don't really mind not rolling around on the floor as a tree in *The Wooden Prince*.

I still undergo extreme mood swings during the course of a day and suffer from a continual undercurrent of loneliness even though I have more friends this season. I am also disgusted at myself for wallowing in self pity when I have so much to be thankful for.

It's a shame the atmosphere in classes and rehearsals has become very tense again. People were much more relaxed after the holidays.

November 1st 1977

Drama at the Düsseldorf Ballet...! Members of the direction have been throwing fits of temper again and receiving opposition from the dancers. The latter are tired and the former are frustrated because there is so little rehearsal time. The problem is that people keep getting sick or injured and time for forthcoming productions is lost preparing new casts. There is a large intake of new dancers this year who have to learn all the ballets. We seldom perform the same production more than twice a month so it is always necessary to rehearse all the productions in advance.

These problems tempt me to think about other companies; I am still very keen to go to Holland. However, I am apprehensive about moving now I am coping better with life here, and I am spoilt by a fat wage packet every month.

December 11th 1977

I have a companion! I've bought myself a sweet green budgerigar. She was very quiet when I first brought her home in her cage, but after a day or two she started chirping and looking livelier. I am very excited about my new little friend. Everyone knows about her and it's easier to invite people to my flat now. I just ask them if they'd like to come and meet my budgie! She will meet my parents soon when they come over to spend Christmas with me.

I saw *Gone with the Wind* for about the third time, and wished I had a Rhett Butler to hold me in his arms.

January 15th 1978

Work has been uneventful. Elsa-Marianne von Rosen is mounting *La Sylphide* for the next premiere. It's an unchallenging piece for the corps de ballet, but she is a nice lady to work with: very calm. She is even managing to remove the tension from the dancers' necks and shoulders. I'm only in Act Two, and I find dieting difficult when I don't have much dancing to do.

I am still enjoying my budgie's chirpy company, and let her fly freely in my room even though she leaves droppings everywhere. The elusive boyfriend remains elusive …

February 20th 1978

I have started lessons with a violinist in the Opera orchestra. The violin is a Christmas present from my father. He has been researching the making of instruments in the violin family for some years now, combining his musical talent with his carpentry skills. The first instrument he made was a cello. This is his first violin. Bored with my "teach yourself" books that I started learning from, I need the stimulation of a teacher. It would be nice if my pitch were as good as my bowing. The neighbours haven't complained yet!

I have discovered a wonderful ballet teacher, Egbert Strolka, who teaches the Pina Bausch Company in Wuppertal and at the school in Essen. His classes are wonderful, such a contrast from the company classes in Düsseldorf, working for correct alignment and control. He has an excellent rapport with the dancers and there are none of the frictions that we experience with our teachers here.

Swan Lake has brought me a new part as a princess in Act Three. This is especially thrilling as it gives me the opportunity to dance with Peter Breuer, a guest principal dancer, who I find very handsome.

April 9th 1978

Well, the unbelievable has happened - I have a boyfriend! How did I meet him you ask, after all those years of wondering how girls meet boys?

Two weeks ago my mother was here and we were on our way to the Opera house in a taxi. The taxi collided with a motorcycle sending the rider flying. I was upset because I had silently anticipated the collision. I felt responsible and was very concerned for the fallen rider. So I gave my name and address to the police as a witness and we continued our journey in another taxi.

The following day a young man turned up at my flat to ask me what I had seen of the accident. It was the motorcyclist. I was so relieved he was alive and unhurt.

A few days later I received a letter from him explaining that he really liked me but had not dared to ask me out when we first met on my doorstep. He asked me out now and thus I had my first ever date! I was a nervous wreck for two days beforehand. It's not the best combination since we are both shy and he doesn't speak any English. It is certainly good for my German. At eighteen, Fritz is a year younger than me. He is a motor mechanic and his big joy in life is his motorbike.

He arrived with a bunch of flowers for my mother and five red roses for me on our first date. As my mother had been with me when he first met me, he presumed we live together. I invited him to a performance and he took me out afterwards. It was pleasant and when he had walked me home I allowed him to kiss me lightly on the lips. I was terribly worried about what would happen and what I should do, but Fritz is very gentlemanly and courteous.

I am not in love, but I appreciate very much having found a polite considerate companion. I feel rather like an intruder on my own romance, as if I'm reading a book; it's all so unreal. As much as I appreciate the thoughtful attention Fritz gives me, I feel like it's all a rehearsal and the performance will follow later.

April 16th 1978
I had to take a couple of days off with a badly upset stomach. I wonder if it was caused by all the recent excitement. A free weekend followed and I went to Holland to see my family there. Fritz was in my thoughts a lot. Mostly I'm unsure about the situation.

My father has definitely retired, and after a lot of hassles a reduced pension has been sorted for him. This is a relief for my parents after living with clouds of uncertainty for a couple of years.

Janet Lewis has invited me to dance the leading part of Swanhilda in a small production of *Coppélia* for the Greenwich Arts Festival in London this summer. It will be so good for me to work on a challenging role and wonderful to dance at home where my friends can come and see me. With plans for a family trip to America going ahead it promises to be an eventful summer.

Rehearsals for the premiere of Walter's *Kalevala* are in progress. It is set to different pieces of Sibelius' atmospheric music including *The Swan of Tuonela*. There will be a soprano singer onstage with us, but there doesn't seem to be clear story line. We are in long bright yellow dresses

34

with orange patches, high neck and long sleeves: I wouldn't buy a night-dress in such bad taste. I can't find much to say about the choreography. The atmosphere can be tense when Walter is unsure about what he wants. I suppose all choreographers are like that.

April 23rd 1978

Last night I dreamed about a gorgeous, cuddly man who was madly in love with me. I woke up feeling antagonistic towards Fritz who does not fit this image. I am a little concerned because I watch the clock when I am with him and look at other men. The novelty he brought into my life has worn off and though I appreciate that he has been very nice to me, I am simply not interested in him. He is disappointed that I will not ride on his motorbike with him. Considering the way we met and that I am a ballet dancer, it is hardly surprising.

April 28th 1978

Whoever would have thought I'd have boyfriend problems! I have been feeling the end was in sight with Fritz for a little while now, but I still gave it a chance. Now I feel like a hypocrite because I like him for what he represents not for himself. I feel almost ashamed of myself to have taken advantage of a nice young German boy who has really been very sweet and charming to me. The trouble is, he going to expect things to develop, whereas I see nowhere for them to go.

This morning I found myself sitting next to an American trombone player during a break in rehearsals at the Opera house canteen. I immediately found him to be warm and humorous. This only confirmed my thoughts that Fritz and I do not belong together. I wonder how tall the trombonist is, I only saw him sitting down - but he did look cuddly! Later I found out that his name is Josh. Apparently he asked what my name is too!

I don't know how to break up with someone, so in addition to telling Fritz I won't ride on his motorcycle with him, I told him I'm too exhausted from work to see him. I hope he gets the message.

April 29th 1978

I met Josh again in the theatre canteen today. He asked me to go for a stroll with him. I'd had two sips of my coffee so I wasn't exactly in a rush, but I decided I had to sacrifice something, so I abandoned the coffee. We went for a short walk around the Opera House, me in my pointe shoes, and he asked me out this evening.

We met at ten, after our respective rehearsals, and went to a wine cellar and disco in the old town. Josh seemed fairly extrovert, yet possibly even more nervous than me. Conversation flowed easily and I learned that he is twenty-seven and comes from Chicago. He has a job in Zurich in Switzerland next season. He is not as chivalrous as Fritz, but he is much more entertaining. He is also much freer with his hands ... I was cautious however. Even though I find him attractive, we went home our separate ways agreeing to meet again tomorrow. I am so relieved to have met someone I find physically attractive.

April 30th 1978

I slept very badly last night, tossing and turning as subtly erotic images of Josh wafted through my dreams. Restless, I got up early, had a bath and washed my hair. As I was early for the appointment with Josh I walked most of the way to our meeting place in Grafenburg on the outskirts of Düsseldorf where he lives. Josh was a few minutes late and I started to panic, afraid he had deserted me.

We went for a long walk in a nearby wood. There was sunshine and a blue sky. I didn't know that there is such a beautiful spot in Düsseldorf. It was so nice to be in the midst of nature.

As we walked chatting away, Josh would hold me subtly in different places and occasionally he would try to kiss me. I shied away telling him I don't like to be "assaulted" in public places, which he found highly amusing. When I was honest with him about my inexperience in these things, he was understanding, though he found it hard to believe.

It was when we got back to his spacious flat and we cuddled on his sofa that I started to succumb. I had wild butterflies in my stomach, but I trusted Josh. Slowly I began to respond. I was afraid I might seem frigid but he was patient and gentle. He is divinely cuddly and I feel cosy and secure in his arms. Fritz's half hearted pecks at my lips gave me no warning of the real thing. Of course I had read about it, but now I know first hand what it's like. The kissing part was the newest and least rewarding for me; something I shall have to get used to. But I adored the cuddling and caressing. I did not think a human being could compete with the soft warmth of my blankets. Now I realise there is no comparison. For once I let myself go, giving in to the impulse of the moment, and I surprised myself. I am still tingling all over.

It's perfectly clear Josh wants to sleep with me, but he knows I'm a virgin and promises not to push me into anything I'm not ready for. I know there is no big future with him, he goes to Zurich next season and has a girlfriend in America. But perhaps a couple of months of fun are better for me at this stage than complicated involvements. I don't think I am going to fall in love with him; I don't know if I'm capable. However, I do find him attractive. He is slightly taller than me, with warm brown eyes, golden hair and a soft beard, and I am crazy about his American accent. Most of all I like the way he responds to me, making me feel beautiful and desirable. I am awakening to sensations I have never experienced before. It is strange that things are suddenly happening to me which I had given up hoping for.

May 8th 1978
Getting to know Josh led to me losing my virginity - or as he puts it: giving it away. It was an enormous emotional and physical relief as I lay weeping silent tears in his arms afterwards. He is a passionate lover as well as being a nice person and I am so lucky to have been able to have such a rewarding first experience. My feet have barely touched the ground recently and I am fired with fresh inspiration in my dancing.

May 20th 1978
The premiere of *Kalevala* seemed to be successful. No-one really understands what it is about; but the music, costumes and decor are apparently very effective together.

It's fun to meet Josh in the interval of a performance, looking very handsome in his tuxedo. It also gives me a thrill to be dancing onstage knowing he is playing in the orchestra. Operas are more enjoyable now also as I can sit in the circle and admire the trombones! My social circle has grown since meeting Josh and I am much happier and more outgoing than before. He persuaded me to buy a companion for my budgie. He didn't think it fair for me to have a mate and my budgie to remain single! So now I have two pairs of wings flapping around my flat.

June 12th 1978
Four girls were called to speak to Erich Walter this morning, including me. We saw him individually but were each told that we should lose weight over the summer or our contracts would not be renewed after next season. I think I surprised him by asking him if he would help me by letting me know when I am thin enough. He gave me the discouraging answer; "you can never be too thin". Of course he is right, I am too fat, the weight has been creeping up and I'm about 54 kilos again. However I have been told by friends and colleagues that I do not look fat onstage. It frightened me to have my security threatened, even though I know it is time I looked around for another job to expand my experience.

This evening I had a phone call to tell me that the date of the *Coppélia* performance in London has been changed and it coincides with our holiday in America. This forces me to make a choice between the two, and after discussing it with my parents I have decided to choose America. I am very disappointed to miss *Coppélia*, but the arrangements are still vague and there is no guarantee the performance will take place.

Life is strange: one day everything can seem perfect and in no time at all it can all crumble at ones feet. I am not cheered by the prospect of Josh leaving soon. He has become a special friend and we've had wonderful times together.

June 20th 1978

I saw Josh off this morning. He took the 7am train to Luxembourg from where he will take his plane to Chicago. He was loaded down with heavy suitcases and trombone cases. We were both in a gloomy mood. For almost two incredibly full months we spent a tremendous amount of time together. His last words to me were, "I'm going to miss you. Ring me when you get to New York". I shall miss him too, but at least I'll always cherish happy memories of our time together. There was no bitterness of a relationship going sour.

I am depressed about my weight and my attempts to diet. Ironically, a decidedly fat, unattractive, and untalented girl was accepted into the company the day after the four girls were ticked off about their weight by Walter. No-one can understand this.

****

I did call Josh when I was in America with my parents, and we had a long chat on the phone. I had a great holiday in the USA, and the performance of *Coppélia* was cancelled. I had long discussions with my father and came to the conclusion that a fourth year in Düsseldorf would be a more harmful risk than a year of unemployment in London. At least in London I could work on my technique and body shape, be artistically stimulated, and be at home near the support of my parents. The hope of course was to get another contract somewhere else.

****

September 6th 1978

It is a relief to have given in my resignation though I am also a little upset about it. I never expected to feel sentimental. New contracts have to be signed by the end of October and I shall not be able to secure another job by then, so I am taking the risk of being unemployed next year. I don't want to stay in Germany, so I'll audition for companies in Holland and Switzerland.

I'm still being ticked off about being out of line and not dancing at the same time as everyone else. How can I give my soul and be an Artist in the corps de ballet when I must concentrate on such things?

We have had exactly the same exercises in class everyday for two weeks. I wonder if this is really effective. Repetition of exercises is supposed to be strengthening, but nothing is achieved when people become bored and frustrated.

I am working hard and dieting to prepare myself for auditions. I'm still homesick. I don't know how to dispel the feeling, but gradually I'm learning to live with it. Having more friends in Düsseldorf helps.

September 13th 1978

This evening I went to a class at the "Werkstatt". I was introduced to this centre a few days ago by a friend who is involved in choreographic workshop performances there. It has been open about six months and offers dance, drama and art classes for adults and children as well as occasional performances. The ones I saw were an eye opener for me as I've seen so little modern dance. I was fascinated by new movements I've never seen before and was interested to see how effectively modern dance can fit with classical music.

I went to a jazz class given by a French dancer and teacher to whom I'd been introduced at the performances. I was rather nervous about the class, having minimal experience of this style. However, I seemed to manage quite well, adapting much more easily than I'd expected, and was complimented on this. I spoke French with Pierre, the teacher, who was most charming to me with his theatrical, chiselled, dark features and warm smile.

I still go to Egbert Strolka's classes in Wuppertal and Essen whenever I can. It is like a breath of fresh air to get away from the company studios and do classes elsewhere.

September 21st 1978

I did class in Essen today and was astounded to bump into Pierre in the corridor. He was also very surprised and invited me for a coffee. He told me about himself. He dances with a small modern group in Essen as well as working at the Werkstatt in Düsseldorf. He is twenty-six, has travelled a lot, has been married and has a daughter. It is clear he finds me

39

attractive and if I am honest with myself I miss the physical comfort I discovered with Josh, and I find it romantic to speak French ...

September 26th 1978

I went to another jazz class yesterday evening and afterwards was invited to join Pierre and some others for dinner. Later everyone went their different ways and Pierre walked me home. As it was very late and the last tram had gone, I suggested he call for a taxi from my flat. I gave him tea and we listened to music. It was three hours before the taxi was ordered. We found we share a tremendous amount of common interests apart from dance.

I admit I had doubts about inviting him up, but Pierre behaved as a perfect gentleman. The most he did was to kneel and kiss my hands as he thanked me for a lovely evening. "We have stolen a little time from Düsseldorf" his silky voice told me, "nothing has changed but us."

September 27th 1978

I think I must be in love ... I've been dancing around my room trying to tire myself even though I had a performance this evening. I'm in such a state of euphoria that sometimes I think I'm overestimating the whole thing. But I just can't help myself, I'm so happy and energetic - I want to shout to the world that I'm in love. Food has suddenly become so unimportant and I can feel I'm getting thinner. Perhaps I'm in love with being in love, but what does it matter so long as I'm happy?

September 30th 1978

Yesterday I decided to go to Essen and do class with Egbert in the afternoon break between rehearsals. I had to make a mad dash for a taxi in order to get to the station in time for the train. Some indefinable force seemed to be propelling me and I kept saying to myself, "I must be crazy, what am I doing?" I realised there was a secret hope of bumping into Pierre again although I didn't like to admit it and persuaded myself that I needed the class.

I was a little disappointed when the class was about to begin and there'd been no sign of him, when suddenly he entered the studio. The prospect of doing the same class as Pierre had appealed to me but I was rather disappointed by his dancing. Considering he only started dancing at nineteen, I suppose it's hardly surprising that his Ballet is poor. He seems awkward in classical movements compared to his natural coordination and quality of movement in contemporary dance.

We agreed to have dinner together in Düsseldorf. After our meal Pierre returned to my flat with me. It was very cosy listening to records, snuggling up together and we didn't want to part. In the end he stayed the night, but I made him sleep on the sofa. How could I do that to him? Predictably I couldn't sleep.

October 8th 1978

I went to Cologne yesterday to do class with the Dutch National Ballet who were on tour there. I cornered Rudi van Dantzig who promised to come and watch me, but in the end he was not able to which was a big disappointment. He suggested I attend the auditions in January.

Pierre is staying with me at the moment as he had to leave his flat suddenly and is having problems finding a new one. He works very long hours and sometimes we see very little of each other. I'm finding him more difficult to get on with than Josh. Perhaps the language barrier is a problem especially when I'm tired and can't think clearly in French. He is also moody and can be very introverted. But I do like to have company.

October 15th 1978

I had a surprise phone call at midnight from Zurich. Josh boasts about his wonderful flat with two balconies overlooking the lake and mountains and I have an open invitation to visit him.

I feel deflated after the class with the Dutch National Ballet and work is uninspiring. I'm a peasant girl in Act One of *Giselle* but apart from that there is nothing new to do. I see less and less of Pierre, he works ridiculously long hours and suffers a lot muscular pains: the price of starting dancing as an adult.

My eating is very erratic, alternate bingeing and starvation. It's no wonder I'm exhausted all the time. I'm going to Egbert's classes a lot which help to keep me going.

November 18th 1978

I went to Amsterdam and did class with Scapino Ballet in the midst of snivels and another bad cold. The director could not come and watch me, but the teacher, who is also his assistant, watched me. I was told that they don't know how many contracts they can offer to foreign dancers because they have to give Dutch dancers priority, but they might contact me.

November 20th 1978

Sometimes, about once a month, life is wonderful. The rest of the time it is a heavy burden that I carry on my shoulders. The solution must be to develop strong shoulders.

December 16th 1978

Like the solitary sheep who has lost his flock
Wandering on the barren hillside through a cold December fog,
Whose only instinct is to survive -
To be reunited with the secure familiarity of the flock:
Thus I drift through life's uncertainties in search of my destiny.

December 20th 1978

The relationship with Pierre is over. An unexpected phone call from Josh this evening gave me the strength I needed to tell Pierre how I feel. His feelings included a lot of hurtful insults to me. Basically we are totally incompatible and perhaps I made a mistake to get involved with him. We had some special moments in the beginning, but they say "love is blind" and in this case it certainly was true. Hopefully it was a mistake I can learn from.

December 27th 1978

Josh phoned again and invited me to stay with him, but I've decided to go home. I need to get my head sorted out; I'm in such a mess at the moment. I faked an injury to get a sick note from a doctor. After limping all the way to the airport I almost believed I had strained my ankle!

February 4th 1979

A month at home did help sort me out emotionally, though I still have a lot of work to do on my body. I had put on weight drastically in December. Although I shed a kilo or so at home, I still have to lose a lot.

On my return to Düsseldorf, I found that about a third of the company had been off with various illness and injuries. They have been rehearsing for a new full evening production by Walter to music by Arnold Schoenburg. I went to the premiere but was disappointed to find it monotonous. I met Egbert in the audience and told him one of the main reasons I had returned to Germany was to do his classes. He didn't believe me but it's quite true. He is a brilliant teacher.

I am breaking into performances again with *Les Sylphides* but there is not much for me to do. We have three free days over the weekend and I'm going to visit Josh in Zurich. It will be strange to see him after seven months. Apparently he has shaved off his beard but assures me he's as handsome as ever! The director of the Zurich Ballet Company told me there are no vacancies when I rang, so it won't be possible to audition there.

February 10th 1979

It was weird to see Josh again and I almost didn't recognise him without the beard. He was a perfect host making me feel very welcome. He showed me around Zurich, and invited me to attend rehearsals and concerts. I enjoyed his beautiful apartment overlooking the lake and mountains just as he had promised. It was a perfect romantic weekend. I like Zurich and loved being in Switzerland which is so familiar from all our summer holidays there. Josh has a huge Volvo into which he disappears in the driving seat and we drove into the mountains one afternoon. It was a glorious day. I inhaled the fresh air deep into my lungs as we walked holding hands in the snow. I regret a little that we don't live closer, especially now he has split from his American girlfriend. We get on so well together.

February 14th 1979

Only a few days later, I have a date here in Düsseldorf. Ryan is a tall, athletically handsome Canadian trumpet player in the orchestra. I've been aware of him for sometime, but warm vibes never passed between us. Today I found myself sitting at the same table as him in the theatre canteen and before lunch was over we had agreed to go to the opera *Salome* this evening. My feelings are mixed because I find him dashingly attractive and I'm sure that's not a good base for getting to know someone.

February 28th 1979

After *Salome* Ryan took me out to the old town. He is very charming, chivalrous, philosophical, honest but tactless, and admits to being self centred. He told me that as long as he remembers me, he will remember that we had our first date on Valentine's Day. I wonder how long that will be … I don't think I'll ever forget him, he's quite swept me off my feet.

At twenty-three Ryan boasts about being a very talented trumpet player, which he is. He is obviously emotionally unsettled and still upset about the recent break up of a long term relationship. Perhaps it is this suffering which gives him an air of maturity. Anyhow we have been spending a lot of time together. He can be moody, but mostly he is entertaining and never boring. One way and another I need not be lonely and that is heaven.

I've been working hard to get myself into decent shape to do auditions during our free week in March.

March 24th 1979

I started my auditions in Munich. I liked the town and found people much friendlier than in Düsseldorf. Lynn Seymour, who is the director there, took part in the class as well as watching. She was friendly, taking my name and address, explaining that she has to see everyone auditioning before making any decisions about contracts.

Next, I went to Basle where Heinz Spoerli politely told me after the class that although I am a nice dancer, I am too "big". I can go back if I lose weight.

Still, I found the courage to return to Scapino Ballet in Amsterdam. This time the director watched class and told me that I am a good dancer with many possibilities but my shape is wrong. The message is coming through loud and clear - I have got to do something about my hips and bottom. Nonetheless, I am encouraged that the directors show interest in me.

The relationship with Ryan is erratic and unpredictable as he is. This can be irritating, but I take each day as it comes and enjoy the good times we spend together.

April 4th 1979

I had to take time off for dropped metatarsals (a minor injury to the foot) which was frustrating and didn't help my diet. But the heat treatment and rest seemed to have cured it. Now I've gone back to class but I feel fat and out of practise. It is as if I am in a long black tunnel and I can't see the end of it. I feel fat, ashamed, guilty and ashamed of my guilt.

I bump into Ryan often at the opera house but there is a rift between us.

April 18th 1979

A visit from my father, and good classes from a guest teacher, have both helped to inspire me and put me back on track again. My father gave me a pep talk, warning me that this is my last chance to pull myself together if I plan on a future in dance. I know he is right; I shall be twenty-one this summer, and this is no longer young for a dancer. Having good company classes for a change has made it a pleasure instead of an ordeal to go to work. The guest teacher, Frau Benador, has such a wonderful understanding of how to tune up a body so that by the end of the class one feels as if one is flying and ready for anything.

April 28th 1979

It is hard to keep on track, but I'm trying. The company has been busy learning László Seregi's *Sylvia*. I am only involved as a cover, so most of my energy goes into classes and practise. I still attend Egbert's classes in Essen and Wuppertal whenever I can. Ryan continues to be moody. Sometimes he is warm towards me, and sometimes he is cool. It's very difficult for me to control my emotions as I care about him and am still in love with him.

May 10th 1979

I have a bad cold and have been written off sick again. I find it hard to concentrate, and my energy ebbs and flows unpredictably. I am having trouble sleeping. In five days I fly to London to audition for Ballet for All, a small group run by John Field which aims to bring classical ballet to smaller venues and towns which otherwise would not be able to see it. I hope I'll also be able to rehearse for *Coppélia* which Janet Lewis is now planning on presenting this year for the Greenwich Arts Festival as last year's project was cancelled. I really feel I need to go back to school for a few months to consolidate my technical foundations and build a reserve of strength on top of them. I have little confidence in my technique right now.

May 24th 1979

The short visit home did me the world of good and I feel like a new person though it is strange to be here, basically marking time till the end of the season. I'm also starting to feel sad at the prospect of leaving my little flat which I have made my home in Germany the last three years.

The audition was almost a repeat of my first Dutch National audition. I was thrown out with a number of others half way through the class, and afterwards when I went to ask John Field the reason he couldn't remember. So I was invited to join another class in the afternoon which I was allowed to finish. Then I was told in the nicest possible way that my hips are "too generous".

I have four weeks to lose three kilos for the performance of *Coppélia*. I just must be strong with myself. I am trying not to think about food and have started learning Spanish as a distraction. I have a ridiculous amount of free time at the moment and I try to occupy myself as much as possible. I've also taken up jogging and occasional timpani lessons from the orchestra timpanist. Ryan and I are still friends, but the romance is over; I refuse to let him upset me any more.

May 31st 1979
Little by little I seem to be adjusting to solitude. I'm spending more time alone than ever before as I have no more rehearsals. My concentration is on packing to go home and keeping myself as fit as I can.

June 3rd 1979
Amazing news! Due to overwhelming demand for tickets, a second performance of *Coppélia* has been put in the evening after the scheduled matinée. One performance would be a challenge, but the prospect of two is frightening as well as exciting.

I am surprised that several men have made advances to me recently, but I am totally closed to them. All my energy is devoted to my work and the return to London.

June 12th 1979
The days seem to drift by as morning becomes night becomes morning … and one day barely seems distinguishable from the next. I seem to be living in a trance like daze. I am trying to keep up discipline to practise, in which I am succeeding, but not without difficulty. And I am always chiding myself for not working more, and not eating less. I am however gaining a greater sense of independence by going out on my own and even getting involved in conversations with strangers. My favourite haunt is the "Irish Pub" and I often meet friends there. It is popular amongst English speaking people and contrasts with the bier cellars and pizza restaurants that overcrowd the old town.

June 13th 1979
I spoke to Josh on the phone this evening. It was so good to hear his voice and hear him sounding happier now he has a new girlfriend. He asked me to not forget him when I am rich and famous. I shall not forget him, even if I am never rich and famous!

June 15th 1979
I am crying tears of spontaneous relief - on the plane to London. I can't analyse them - I am just feeling, and suddenly the world is so beautiful. The sky is such magnificent colours I should like to paint it.

Chapter Three

London - Dublin   1979 - 1980

June 18th 1979

My new life has started at such a speed I've had no time or energy to think about it. I dived straight into rehearsals with Janet Lewis. Gradually I'm beginning to get inside the character of Swanhilda, but it disturbs me that it is so difficult for me to forget the steps and get on with the acting. I find it hard to leave myself behind and step into the part without inhibition in the presence of the rest of the cast, though everyone is most helpful. It's so rewarding to be able to get my teeth into constructive work again after all those wasted months in Düsseldorf. I have a few doubts about my ability to handle the role of Swanhilda, but every confidence that Janet will get the best possible performance from me.

June 21st 1979

Rehearsals have been going better and I am feeling much more confident. We had a run through at the theatre today. The raked slope of the stage did not bother me too much, but sometimes it's like climbing Mount Everest when I dance upstage towards the backdrop. Generally, it is the older theatres which have a raked stage; the modern ones in which I performed in Germany had flat stages.

I've had bleeding blisters on my toes every day from the intense pointe work and dancing with the constant pain from them is tiring, but Janet's energy and enthusiasm do wonders to keep up my inspiration. Basically I'm optimistic despite my figure problems. I've succeeded in losing some weight, but I don't look right yet.

My twenty-first birthday passed uneventfully. I feel I am still so young, on the threshold of life, yet I know time is running out if I hope to achieve anything in my dancing career.

June 24th 1979

Another milestone; my first principal role. It was a marathon day with a hard class and two performances, but I survived despite an excruciatingly sore blister. In the beginning I was nervous, and uncomfortable, but by the second act in the matinée I was able to lose myself in the dancing. The first act in the evening went really well and there were moments when technique, interpretation, partner and music came together in a fantastic way that has never happened for me before. There were a number of times when I felt I was flying.

This evening I tasted the fruit of being a ballerina. It tasted good and I could handle it. This gives me all the confidence and inspiration I need to get myself and my body in order.

July 11th 1979

I have been having a lot of nightmares since I left Germany, but it is beautiful to be home again. Despite my precarious situation, I don't feel insecure. I feel cosy, inspired, positive, determined and happy. I saved money in Germany and cashed in a German pension plan, so I am able to live on that. My weight is under better control now, and I am working hard in open classes in London with excellent teachers such as Maryon Lane and Eileen Ward, and in coaching sessions with Janet. I'm going to stay at home for three weeks whilst my parents go on holiday to Switzerland. I was going to accompany them, but then I realised that I need work and discipline, not a holiday.

July 22nd 1979

I can't believe I weigh 50 kilos. At last I'm starting to look like a dancer. I still need to tone up my muscles and overcome my addiction to diuretics, but I'm definitely going in the right direction and haven't taken an appetite suppressant since I was home. I can't see the difference in my reflection in the mirror but my clothes are hanging off me, so I must be thinner. I have to keep working hard at it.

In my parents' absence, I am experiencing a period of tranquility and contentment, perfectly satisfied to spend time totally alone with the cat as my companion. My dancing is totally absorbing me.

August 8th 1979

I'm feeling very deflated after this morning's audition for London Festival Ballet. It was held on the stage of the Royal Festival Hall where the company is performing this month. We were seen in small groups (about 8 to 10 at a time) for half an hour of classwork. The auditions went on all day as there were about a hundred hopeful applicants for one or two places. We were told we would be contacted if they were interested in us; but that is what they always say. It is most disheartening.

September 26th 1979

I had an incredible nightmare. The whole thing was unreal; like watching a film you get involved with as if you are experiencing it, but you know that it's not really happening to you.

It all started in a theatre. I saw myself alone in the wings watching everyone else dancing onstage. I was not onstage because I was fat. I felt wretched and was crying bitterly. The dream moved through various scenes which are already blurred in my memory, but there was a very tense atmosphere. Then suddenly two men appeared with a pair of giant scissors and moved towards me. My throat seized as I heard myself scream "stop the film - the dream's over!" I started running out of the room we were in and down some stairs. The men pursued me and as they neared, realising there were another ten or so flights of stairs before I reached safety, I created a window in my imagination and jumped out still shouting "the dream's over". I forced myself to wake up.

The message in the dream is clear. I feel outcast if I'm fat, and I fear losing my chance to dance because of it.

November 15th 1979

At the beginning of October I suffered a severe attack of cramp which kept me in bed for five days and away from classes for a month. I was rushed to hospital with a suspected collapsed lung and prodded by various specialists. This only aggravated the pain. An osteopath diagnosed air in the stomach and with time it disappeared. I suspect that years of taking diuretics might have affected me and promised myself to stop taking them. Miraculously I managed not to gain weight whilst sedentary and it seems to have settled at 49 kilos. I am finding my diet discipline.

Now I'm desperately working to get back into shape for auditions in Holland next month. I'm surprised how quickly I'm gaining strength after being off for so long. The osteopath recommended Pilates body conditioning to me, and I'm sure that my progress is due to this and working carefully. I'm fired with enthusiasm since Janet has asked me to go to Ireland as principal dancer for six months when she takes over a young company in Dublin in the New Year.

December 3rd 1979

In Europe to go and do auditions in Holland, it's nice to see my friends, but strange to be back in Germany. Düsseldorf is like a diamond; it glitters glamorously, but the edges cut. Arriving from London I am struck afresh by the abundance of wealth. The quality and style of the abundant chic shops in the Könings Allee is overwhelming. And all the furs … I used to see it so often I took it all for granted. However people do not talk to each other here. No-one strikes up a conversation in a supermarket queue as they might in London. Everything is impersonal and grey. I really hope I never have to live anywhere like this again.

December 11th 1979

At least I had the satisfaction of finishing the audition for the Dutch National Ballet and not being thrown out in the middle. However, when I asked Rudi van Dantzig what was wrong with me, I received the reply "you don't have the style we are looking for". There is no answer to that. Bitterly disappointed I called my parents to tell them what had happened. Scapino Ballet had held their audition the same day a few hours later and I had missed it. My parents persuaded me to go and do a class with them the following day.

When I turned up at Scapino's studios on the outskirts of Amsterdam I was told the audition had been held the previous day. Armando Navarro, the director, did however come to watch the class; he remembered me. Afterwards he told me that they were terribly sorry but there were no more contracts.

I was on my way out of the building when I was called back to the office. I was told that they were very impressed by how hard I must have worked to lose weight and get into such good shape. On the strength of this they wanted to offer me a contract which was supposed to be going to another girl, but had not yet been promised to her. I would have to dance with Scapino 10, the smaller group of the company, but would have more solo opportunities working with this group than with the larger one. This did not satisfy my dream of dancing with the Dutch National Ballet, but if offered me security and the chance to live in Amsterdam where I could always try again. So I accepted.

February 4th 1980

Impatient to start work with so much to look forward to, January dragged, but at last I am in Ireland staying in Janet's house till I find a flat. I shall share with an Australian dancer, who has come over from England with us. The house is damp and I'm very cold so I've been extravagant and bought myself an electric fire.

We travelled from London on a rickety old train from Euston to Holyhead, and then on a boat from there to Dun Laoghaire. We were warmly greeted on our arrival and made to feel most welcome.

My first impressions of Ireland are of rain and familiarity: cars driving on the left-hand side of the road, English language around me, and English products in the shops. Rain seems to pour all the time, and when it doesn't it looks as if it's about to. It feels like being in another part of England rather than being abroad.

We rehearse in a church hall. It's very cold and damp, but we've been promised a heater. The standard of the company is low; I'm certainly strong enough to be their principal dancer. Everyone has been very friendly.

February 10th 1980

The Australian dancer and I have found a maisonette in Dun Laoghaire. It is light and cheerful by day and cosy by night. There are many windows with views over the rooftops and distant hills. We even have a glimpse of the sea. The bathroom is off the entrance hall and the living room, kitchen and two small bedrooms are upstairs.

Transport by local buses is primitive and they break down regularly. It takes about an hour to get to the hall in Sandymount just eight kilometres away. This whole area around Dublin is built up as the most densely populated area of Southern Ireland. Everything is the complete opposite of Germany. The working conditions leave much to be desired, but the company has the luxury of its own theatre in Dun Laoghaire; so no competition with the opera company for performances. Also, in contrast to Germany, my work is valued here, and I have companionship. There is no need for me to feel lonely. Everyone is so calm and friendly. No-one would dream of shouting at the dancers here.

The company performs contemporary and jazz ballets as well as classical ones. Thus, in addition to ballet class every morning, there are two Martha Graham technique contemporary classes and two jazz classes every week. I am in agony with sore muscles from the latter techniques which my body is not accustomed to. We work six days a week here, whereas in Germany we worked five days.

February 12th 1980

I dreamed of Ryan last night, so clearly. It was uncanny.

March 2nd 1980

I've been exploring the coast and lovely walks along the cliff tops. The air is so fresh here. I still can't believe I live by the sea.

Work is going well and I'm feeling much stronger than when I did *Coppélia* last summer. It's very nice to have the chance to work on it all again. I am lucky that Christian Addams, who partners me, is very strong

51

and experienced. He is also giving us very good classes; nice and slow so we can find our placing.

We had a photo call for the programme and when I saw the proofs I was amazed how sleek I look. It's such a relief and pleasure to be a respectable shape at last. With continued discipline I'm maintaining my 49 kilos.

March 7th 1980

As the performances approach I am getting quite excited. I realise I have a lot of responsibility as my dancing can help or hinder the overall success of this young company, Dublin City Ballet. But I'm not wasting too much thought on that; I'm far too busy getting to know my character of Swanhilda. Self assured and mischievous she dominates the action, especially in the second act where she tricks Dr Coppelius into believing that his favourite doll, *Coppélia*, has come to life. I think about her a lot and can hardly wait to get onstage and share her fun with the audience.

This evening there was a press reception at the Shelbourne Hotel which is one of Dublin's chic, expensive ones. We had to wear costumes and photographs were taken for various newspapers. I was in demand as the "leading lady" and everyone thought the costumes were very pretty.

March 9th 1980

We rehearsed at the Pavilion Theatre at Dun Laoghaire today. It was fun to be there but it took all day before I felt at home on the raked stage. I am getting into the spirit of Swanhilda with more ease now but there is still work to be done to get the technique as strong as steel simultaneously with the characterisation. Janet is always marvellous to work with, and I am excited for her in her new role as artistic director; it suits her well. She has arranged the timetable for next week so I have no time to be nervous. I have to go to Sandymount everyday to rehearse the *Nutcracker* pas de deux with Christian as well as having class onstage in the morning and performing in the evening at Dun Laoghaire. This means a lot of dancing and a lot of travelling.

March 11th 1980

The opening night was a fantastic success. Anne Coutrney's jazz ballet was much appreciated and *Coppélia* was a big hit with the audience. I managed not to get too nervous, remaining detached and in control. I was very aware of the audience and for the first time experienced my ability to influence it. We aroused laughs and spontaneous applause, and it was all most rewarding despite my sore feet towards the end.

I was touched to receive so many good luck cards from members of the company. I was also complimented many times on my dancing. We celebrated the triumph at a reception afterwards. It was an achievement to be proud of considering the entire production had been put together in just five weeks.

March 13th 1980

There have been very positive reviews in the press which all said extremely nice things about me. For example The *Irish Times* (11/03/1980) said that my interpretation of Swanhilda was "… full of fun …" and " … technically accomplished". *In Dublin* (March 1980) compared my dancing to a "…. young gazelle." I am quite swept off my feet by it all.

Now we have started on *Nutcracker* Act Two and I'm in love with the music, though I feel quite shattered. I'm not used to working so long and hard on performance days, or to performing every night. My muscles are crying for a break and are agony first thing in the morning. I have to force myself to get out of my cosy bed and then do exercises and stretches before leaving the house to go to morning class. More limbering before class starts, and once I start to perspire during the exercises at the barre my body begins to feel oiled up; ready to execute the demanding tasks of a full day of rehearsals and performances ahead. My feet are surviving, though they usually hurt when I put my pointe shoes on. Then I forget about them because I have to. But I love the work, and can feel my strength growing as I fight through the pain and fatigue.

The audience is different every night; always a packed house. I project myself out across the footlights and am greeted with warm applause. People have already said it is a shame I shall be leaving in the summer. But I know I must leave, I need the competition and stimulation of an established company.

March 15th 1980

Considering the heavy workload I have this week, I have done well, but this afternoon something went wrong causing a black cloud to hang over me.

Paula Hinton was here to watch the performances as she is coming to mount *Eaters of Darkness* for us, which was choreographed by her recently deceased husband Walter Gore. Because of this the second cast danced the principal roles at the matinée giving as many opportunities to different people as possible. I danced the part of a friend exchanging places with the girl who danced Swanhilda. I made an absolute mess of the friends' dance in Act One. Perhaps I was so wound up in the role of

Swanhilda I couldn't do anything else. I only had a couple of rehearsals and I'm sure I didn't use them as I should have done. It didn't occur to me that I might have a problem. I was saving my energy for my other parts: the principal ones. It was a very embarrassing experience and I feel dreadful for letting Janet down. It was also frightening as I totally lost control for a few seconds. The evening performance was intense for me. I felt devastated before I'd even started.

Perhaps it was a good thing to have happened. It was humbling to be reminded that I am not a true professional yet. I still have a great deal to learn.

March 17th 1980
We have a few free days now to recover from all the recent work. I am totally deflated. My flatmate's girlfriend is visiting and though she is a very nice person, the atmosphere we had created as flatmates is intruded on. Perhaps I am slightly envious that he has a companion and I don't.

March 20th 1980
Back at rehearsals, today I made my first attempt at the Sugar Plum Fairy variation from *Nutcracker*. Janet didn't understand why I wasn't able to achieve the required technical brilliance even though I only just started learning it. Unfortunately my mind assimilates new things considerably faster than my body. Later we had a chat and she expressed her shock and disappointment in my dancing at the Saturday matinée. Paula Hinton was not impressed either and I have probably lost my chance of a role in *Eaters of Darkness*. I was also told I need to work more on my technique and placing.

I feel I must be lacking determination. I know I have enormous physical problems, and still cannot really feel the muscles in the pelvis and abdominal regions properly. I think I could be more disciplined about working harder. I just have to learn to transcend the pain and fatigue. Perhaps I am doomed to be in agony the rest of my life, but if I have accepted to be a dancer then I must learn to live with it.

Is it really worth it? I ask myself. How will I even know if I don't try?

March 24th 1980
A few drops of blood suggested a hint of a period. The first reminder of being a woman for almost a year. Perhaps this also explains why I've been feeling so heavy in my thighs, tired, depressed and bloated. Maybe it even explains the lapse in concentration at that fateful matinée performance. When I told Janet, she actually jumped on it as an excuse for me

being out of sorts recently. I was very touched by the realisation of her concern for me and loyalty.

April 1st 1980
I am seeing the light at the end of the tunnel and inspiration is returning. I am enjoying *Nutcracker*. The pas de deux was supposed to finish with a high lift, but when we tried the first time Christian's hand slipped under my ribs causing me a lot of pain. So a floor bound ending was substituted. My left ribs are still very sore, but I am treating them with heat and ointment and they should heal themselves.

April 3rd 1980
We had another press reception last night. It was boring until we were asked to pose outside the hotel in our costumes. The passing motorists found this very amusing.

My ribs still hurt a lot especially in the mornings. They are painful until I get warmed up and perspiring. But I cannot give up, there is no-one to replace me. Nonetheless, I enjoy dancing and my technique is getting stronger.

April 9th 1980
Another first night is over. It was a close shave with two runs on stage yesterday, a dress rehearsal this afternoon and the last costumes arriving just before curtain up. They were building the sets until the last minute too. Everyone felt either under rehearsed, or was nervous about something difficult they had to do. All the stops were pulled out to make another triumphant success.

I became possessed by an indefinable inspiration. It was thrilling and made all the traumas of the last weeks worthwhile. It was amazing how much easier things felt. This really is the beginning. I have so much work ahead of me, but it is wonderful to have something to get my teeth into. Janet was pleased with me. Now I am looking good and working well; I am 47 - 48 kilos. Sometimes I feel weak, but I eat before dancing to give me energy.

April 10th 1980
We had more enthusiastic reviews. The *Irish Independent* (10/04/1980), for example, reported that I danced "…with elegance yet with warmth and individual quality … " Wow!

The bruise on my ribs has come out with arnica ointment and is considerably less painful. It is more of an inconvenience than a major problem now, although last week was tough and I was I tears several times from the pain and tiredness. Christian is a considerate partner and tries to touch the painful areas as little as possible in the pas de deux.

May 7th 1980

It was wonderful to have my father here for two weeks and take his motorbike "taxi service" to work. He came here on his motorbike which, for him, is a comfortable means of travel. He saw several performances. My mother was able to come over for a few days as well to see me dance *Nutcracker*.

My ribs seemed cured but my energy was drained, and when I kept bursting into tears for no apparent reason and coughing a lot, my father insisted on taking me to a hospital. An X-ray revealed that a rib had been cracked though it was healing itself now. I should have worn some sort of support to aid the healing process but it's too late now. Also the injury caused an infection on my lung so I was prescribed antibiotics to clear it. With no space for injured dancers in her company, Janet was not sympathetic. "You are delicate aren't you!" was her response to the news.

The entire company has improved through the season of performances, and finally I conquered the fear I was experiencing every time before the *Nutcracker* pas de deux. At one performance half way through the Waltz of the Flowers, which precedes it, the taped music suddenly stopped. The dancers continued admirably in the silence until the curtain was lowered. Apparently, a fuse had blown and there was a ten-minute break to sort this out. After that the curtain rose on the pas de deux. Rather than making me nervous, this incident helped me to relax as I thought to myself "nothing I do now can be as bad as what just happened".

Dublin City Ballet was invited to Galway where we had a wonderfully warm audience and again encouraging reviews, which mentioned my " … slender limbs and beautiful expressive hands…" (*The Connacht Tribune* 02/05/1980).

My father met me in Galway on his motorbike having watched the performance, and we spent the four free days which followed touring Connemara and the south of Ireland on his bike. I found the former barren and preferred the colours of the Wicklow Mountains near Dublin.

Another new experience for me was a radio interview. I was whisked out of class one day and taken to the recording studio. I was most impressed by the cool efficiency of the presenter. It was a live broadcast and timing was vital. I was in a good mood so I told them all about the special and magical things in Ballet.

May 10th 1980

I had to wait four hours for an X-ray, but at least I know everything is in order now. I have no more pain from the rib, just muscle soreness after four days off.

Anthony Van Laast came to watch a jazz class and has shown interest in using some of us in a film for which he is choreographing the dances.

There is a full house at the flat again with my flatmate's mother from Australia and his girlfriend visiting. It can be a little claustrophobic, but I seek refuge in my room and am relieved not to be lonely. However, there is a void in my life; I long to be in love, even if only in a fantasy. I am thankful to have my work under control and every day the discipline becomes a little easier to switch on. In fact, my body seems to relish the torture I put it through. The improvement in my technique is rewarding and a dream of mine is coming true to dance the role of Odette in *Swan Lake* Act Two. I expect my social life will sort itself out in Holland.

May 18th 1980

The weather is glorious, lots of sunshine at last, but I don't get much chance to see it as I'm working all the time. At least the warmer weather makes it easier to get my body going in the mornings.

Yesterday I went into Dublin's town centre and had a walk in Phoenix Park. I enjoyed watching two elegant swans on a pond giving me inspiration for *Swan Lake*.

May 19th 1980

Another hectic week commences and I dance Swanhilda every morning at the Pavillion Theatre in Dun Laoghaire in performances for schools, and then go to Sandymount to rehearse in the afternoons. The second cast Swanhilda is injured so I have to do all the performances.

Paula Hinton has arrived and auditioned us for the principal roles in *Eaters of Darkness*. To my delight, despite the mishap when she watched performances, I have been chosen to learn the leading female role. It is an energetic and very dramatic ballet and I can't wait to bury myself in it. I adapt to Walter Gore's choreography fairly easily; it is not unlike that of Erich Walter.

May 21st 1980

There has been a change in plans - nothing unusual in this profession - and it has been decided that Paula Hinton will dance the lead in *Eaters of Darkness*. It's a practical solution as there really is very little time to put the piece together. I'm not too disappointed as I'll be able to concentrate my energy into *Swan Lake*.

It's amazing to watch Paula dancing the role of the woman. The steps become so unimportant as one is aware only of the emotions through the development of the plot. Apparently, it is taken from a historical case of a young bride who was wrongly committed to an insane asylum by her husband. She is raped by one of the inmates who also murders another inmate who has befriended the woman. She then murders her assailant having become mad herself through the ordeals of the situation.

May 27th 1980

I'm starting to feel restless as I near the end of my contract here. I look forward to commencing a new life in Amsterdam, and I've been teaching myself Dutch which should help. However, I'm not looking forward to dancing in the corps de ballet after being in the limelight here, though I have to admit the pressure can be quite daunting sometimes.

I'm dancing Swanhilda again, at the Olympia Theatre in Dublin. It is satisfying to have got the technique sufficiently under control in *Coppélia* for it to be a means of expression. I'm no longer nervous about the pirouette turns which used to trouble me. However, I'm forever battling with the whims of my temperamental body and continue to suffer from aching muscles. At night I drop into bed exhausted, and on Saturdays I often sleep through thirteen hours.

June 3rd 1980

I just had a bath and saw myself fully exposed in the mirror giving me quite a shock. My legs look like giraffe necks; I've never been so badly bruised. I was unaware during the filming today that I was getting so many knocks from the actor's armour. It was a long day. I was up at 5.30am to catch a bus at 6.30am in Dun Laoghaire. We were driven out to the location in the countryside and spent the morning in wardrobe and make-up and waiting around.

We were in a banquet scene in John Boorman's *Excalibur* about King Arthur and the Knights of the Round Table. The dancing was simple, but we were supposed to look earthy, not like ballet dancers at all as we pranced around with the soldiers. That was more difficult.

Filming started before lunch and the first shot was completed after a few takes. Lunch was a welcome break. We worked solidly through the afternoon finishing at 5pm. Everyone was very pleased as the scene was ready after one day of filming instead of the predicted two. I shall be paid for two days work and will earn as much for this as I do in a month on my dancer's salary. After all that I performed Swanhilda this evening.

June 10th 1980

This week the *Nutcracker* programme makes a welcome break from *Coppélia* and I'm surprised how much stronger I am than when I did it before. My legs feel like jelly sometimes, I am so exhausted, but my technique has improved. One evening I was thrown flowers from the balcony when I took my curtain call. I have also received fan mail and it is gestures like this which make it all worthwhile.

We continue to rehearse *Swan Lake* in the afternoons. I do a lot of arm and back exercises to try and make myself more swan like. I have a tremendous respect for the role of Odette and I hope I can do it justice.

There are injuries and illnesses amongst the dancers which in Düsseldorf would have been sufficient for two weeks off. Nonetheless, people are valiantly working on. The situation is unsettled and plans for the company are vague. I am envied as I have another job to go to.

June 16th 1980

I am having difficulty getting into the role of Odette. Perhaps it is because I am so tired and my emotions are confused. I have to express love, but I find myself unable to do so. I think I feel guilty about love affairs last year and am afraid to open myself as Odette who must portray love and passion, because my lurid past will reveal itself through my interpretation.

June 26th 1980

The performances last week passed by in a thick fog. I'm too tired, too numb to feel any more emotion. Janet seems satisfied with my interpretation of Odette but I regret being too worn out to be able to enjoy dancing a role which means so much to me.

The *Evening Herald* (24/06/1980) fortunately didn't notice my fatigue as apparently Christian, my partner, and I "… give beautifully controlled performances." I'm thankful to have a month's holiday at home to recharge before I go to Amsterdam.

Chapter Four

Amsterdam   1980 - 1983

August 13th 1980

At last I am in Amsterdam, and it all feels like a dream. I have been so restless, waiting to start my new life here. I am staying with my friend Emma, who recently retired from the Dutch National Ballet, and her husband. They live on the two lower floors of their large house in an older part of the town near the Vondel Park, and rent out the two higher floors.

A Dutch cousin, took me out to dinner this evening to welcome me to Amsterdam. It's so cosy to have people I know around; friends and relatives. I start work with my first class tomorrow. I can't wait.

August 14th 1980

The first class with Scapino Ballet was a gentle one, breaking us into work after the holidays; though I have been attending classes in London. I only stopped dancing for a few days when I had a bad cold. The atmosphere is so friendly, completely different from Düsseldorf.

I started flat hunting today and the situation looks grim. The agencies I went to advised me that flats are very expensive. My best chance is to look for a room with shared bathroom and kitchen facilities.

August 16th 1980

My first day of rehearsals yesterday was a shock to the system. We work through the day from 10am to 5pm with the occasional ten-minute break. However, evenings are free, unless there is a performance. Everyone speaks English so it seems unlikely my Dutch will ever become fluent. It feels strange being new in the company, like a fish out of water, but I expect I shall settle down in time.

I felt more relaxed in class and rehearsals today, but to my absolute horror I have to do a forward roll in one of the ballets. My straight spine makes such movements extremely difficult for me and, ever since gym lessons at school, I have a deep fear of them. I solved the problem at school by arranging to have my piano lessons during gym, but there is no way I can avoid it now. The ballet mistress was sympathetic and tried to help by asking a male dancer to turn me over. Recently I learned to master the shoulder stand; I am determined to overcome the forward roll as well. Apart from this, everything I have to do is well within my capabilities.

August 21st 1980

Acquainting myself with Amsterdam I've been to a concert, explored the museums and walked miles amongst the canals and quaint old houses. One of the best aspects is that it is a cultural centre. The Dutch National Ballet and Nederlans Dans Theater perform here regularly and there are also visiting companies. I'm restless and look forward to settling down to a routine in my own place. I see a lot of my Dutch cousin and he took me to the birthday party of an old school friend of his, in the country south of Amsterdam. Hein, his friend, was rather reserved, but I enjoyed conversations with other people and felt on holiday as it was a lovely sunny day.

Emma has a big colour television set on which she receives BBC2. She can also watch German programmes. It still sends shivers down my spine to hear German; memories of lonely evenings. It is such a relief that people do not raise their voices here at Scapino. I'm glad to be in the smaller group as I'm definitely getting more to do than I would in the larger one. In fact I dance all day almost nonstop, and I love it. I am impressed by the efficient professionalism of the ballet mistress.

After continuing my search for somewhere to live, it appears I shall be remaining in Emma's house. One of the floors upstairs is going to be vacant and I am allowed to have it, provided I find someone to share with and promise not to fight with them! I'm delighted as I will be able to have a large room with a huge balcony overlooking the garden. The kitchen and bathroom are spacious with modern fittings and will be shared with the occupant of the other room. Unfortunately it will not be available until late autumn as it needs redecorating when the current occupants leave. My Dutch cousin has offered to let me stay with him until it is ready. It's certainly a relief to have found somewhere, even if I have to wait for it.

August 26th 1980

I'm feeling more settled now. I enjoy not having the pressure of responsibility hanging over me as in Ireland, and it is wonderful to have relatives here. I'm also making friends in the company. Nonetheless, after the challenges in Dublin I don't feel stretched enough in my work. I have started making sculptures from clay with a wire armature of small dancing figures. This gives me a creative outlet.

September 9th 1980

We have started work on a ballet about a shy scarecrow. No doubt it is a good subject for audiences of children, but it's not very stimulating for dancers. Unfortunately Scapino has quite a lot of ballets in its repertoire which are supposed to be entertaining for children but are unchallenging for the performers.

I am a little homesick sometimes and miss my parents, but distraction is always close at hand and it's hard to remain depressed for long. My forward roll is progressing slowly but I am still nervous about it. Back exercises help to keep my lower spine strong and supple, but part of the problem is that I bruise my boney vertebrae on the hard floor and it hurts to practise the roll.

When I returned to my Dutch cousin's flat this evening the canals were packed with police and inquisitive onlookers clicking their cameras. The police were wearing helmets and were armed with shields and batons. The scene was quite frightening. Apparently, they were removing squatters from a house situated near the flat. It was noisy all evening and we had to close the windows because of tear gas. This morning everything was calm and back to normal.

September 17th 1980

My debut with Scapino Ballet is over. I feel totally disorientated and deflated. The theatre was very small and cramped, and not at all suitable for dance, though it had an intimate atmosphere. It was a charity performance for handicapped children and there was satisfaction in knowing the pleasure we were giving. I was nervous simply because my part was easy. The problems were the predictable ones that arise when one prances around under a sheet and can hardly see anything through the eye holes. I did the best I could and gave my ghost the same concentration and commitment I would give to Odette. In a way it was frustrating, but on the other hand I need only remind myself of the terror of doing something really difficult and it is easier to relax and enjoy life.

September 28th 1980

I'm more optimistic after today's performance in the vast modern, cultural centre in Amstelveen nearby, though I felt very out of place taking my bow in the back row under a sheet. It's a big let down after being the ballerina in Dublin. I tell myself "this isn't me, it's a ghost". I wait quietly for my chance, determined that it will come.

When we tour (this means any performance which is not in Scapino's own studio theatre) we are given a cash allowance in a brown envelope. I have decided to save all my envelopes and open them at Christmas as a treat. I'm able to live on my salary, but it's considerably lower than it was in Germany.

October 1st 1980

We are in Zutphen, about two hours coach ride from Amsterdam and are staying in a hotel two nights in order to present four performances for audiences of school children who are brought to the theatre. The hotel is pleasant and the theatre is a spacious modern one. I am under the sheet again so it amounts to a paid holiday for me. Zutphen is a nice town to wander through with a quaint historical centre.

October 19th 1980

I'm becoming increasingly frustrated with being a ghost; no-one has seen my face onstage yet. There are promises of better things to come around the corner, but nothing has materialised. Waiting to move into my new home is also annoying. It's still in the process of being painted. My sculptures continue to bring satisfaction. It's so rewarding to mould the figures into extraordinary positions I can't do myself with gymnastic high leg extensions and deep back bends.

October 27th 1980

At last I've shown my face onstage, but with only one performance of *Songfest* scheduled, when will it be seen again? It was such a thrill to put my make-up on again, and I enjoyed the performance so much. It was a long day: class from 11am till 12.15pm, a three hour bus trip to Winterswijk near the German border, rehearsal before the show, followed by a three hour return journey afterwards arriving back in Amsterdam after 1am. *Songfest*, with music by Leonard Bernstein and choreography by Ricardo Nunez, is an interesting ballet to perform consisting of songs which tell different stories, creating varied moods. It is artistically challenging and requires dramatic interpretation.

November 3rd 1980

At last I am in the house where I shall live, but I still feel as if I'm camping. I'm living in Emma's spare bedroom and using the kitchen and bathroom upstairs which are ready. The end of the tunnel is in sight, but more patience is necessary. I'm not sure when I'll be able to move into my room.

The dreaded cold has claimed me as a victim yet again. It seems to be going round the company. This is one occasion when I'm thankful not to have a lot of dancing in the performances.

November 13th 1980

Doing my tourist jaunt in Delft is a pleasure. Again I benefit from being under a sheet and not having to put on make-up. Thus I can wander around this famously pretty town in the break between the two shows. I'm certainly seeing a lot of Holland.

November 14th 1980

Two performances of *Songfest* today gave me the satisfaction of putting on my false eye lashes and feeling like a dancer. I'm becoming more and more annoyed with the ghost which I still have to do regularly. If my forward roll and cartwheels were better I might have had a chance of doing *Concerto Grosso* in which they appear, but I was trained as a ballet dancer, not an acrobat. This is a lesson in patience I suppose.

November 17th 1980

I had my first experience of a demonstration performance in a school today. The children were quieter and more attentive than they often are in the theatres. The choreography is enjoyable and reasonably challenging to dance. It requires versatility: from a languorous solo on pointe, to a disco routine for the trio of dancers in each group. We travel with a technician who lays down a special dance floor and is in charge of the sound equipment, and someone from the education department who introduces the dances to the audience. Usually we are left alone and responsible for our work, whereas someone from the management always accompanies us to public performances. This work in the schools is like heaven after life under the sheet!

November 20th 1980

We continue to be busy with school demonstrations this week. Sometimes we have been able to have lights which give a touch of theatricality. It's fun to go off in a van as an individual rather than an anonymous member of a group. Also, I always feel we give the children something positive and entertaining. It is satisfying to see their smiling faces.

The future looks brighter as I shall be promoted from a ghost to the soloist role of the governess who takes a group of children to the haunted castle. I am taking over the part next month from a girl who is leaving. She leaves many parts behind which have been promised to me. Also, I'm cast in a contemporary piece by Charles Czarney for one man and four women to be shown at Christmas. The music is minimalist and we have to count the entire twenty minutes. The choreography is inspired by Tai Chi movements and is danced barefoot - a first for me.

November 26th 1980

We are in Winterswijk for three nights. I'm under the sheet again but enjoying myself anyway. My hotel room has become home, my workshop for sculpting and a place to entertain my colleagues. The figurines are much admired and several people want to buy them from me. There is a good atmosphere amongst the dancers and one evening we invaded a discotheque and relieved the tension of performance.

November 29th 1980

Arriving back in Amsterdam I found a distraught Emma who told me the house had been burgled. Jewellery had been stolen as well as her video recorder and some personal tapes which were precious to her. Miraculously nothing of mine had been taken.

We had a free day today and I went to take class with Nederlands Dans Theatre in The Hague. But I found myself doing an audition instead, which had not been my intention. Even though there were many people, everyone was given a fair chance to be seen. Several dancers from Scapino were there. We were told the old story that we would be contacted if they were interested in us. I plucked up the courage to speak to Jiri Kylian, the director, and express my admiration for his ballets and desire to dance in them. I am sure he appreciated this, but he was not convinced that I might be a prospective member of his company.

December 4th 1980

After a friendly interview with the management in which I was complimented on my work and promised solo and principal parts in the future, as well as a generous pay rise, I decided to stay a second year at Scapino.

December 7th 1980

At long last I am in my room after a hectic few days moving in and organising things. I have been provided with an enormous king size bed in which I am lost on my own, and have been able to buy furniture from the people who were living here before. It is a beautiful room, especially as the paintwork is fresh for me, and I'm so happy to have it. It was definitely worth waiting for.

My flatmate is with the Dutch National Ballet. I was spellbound by her dancing when I watched her in a performance. Thought she is only 1.52 meters tall, she fills every corner of the stage with an inspired presence. Her movements flow with precision, ease and musicality. I feel quite honoured to share with such a talented young lady. To my amazement she is barely twenty.

Yesterday evening I went out with my Dutch cousin and a friend of his who I've known superficially for some time as our families are friends. It was a romantic sort of evening with the first snowfall of this year floating down at midnight. The outing had a strange effect on me because I find this chap attractive and am reminded of the cuddles and affection which are absent from my life at the moment.

I've started performing the role of the governess after twenty-seven appearances under a sheet. Needless to say my new part is considerably more satisfying.

December 15th 1980

I'm a little concerned because I feel so disorientated. I float through life in a trance a lot of the time. It has taken discipline not to gain weight during the last months, but one way or another I'm keeping it steady at about 49 kilos. However, I have started the diuretics again which really do me no good at all. The truth is, the way I look is more important than the way I feel. Occasionally I get cramps and I know I must break this bad habit.

A discussion with colleagues revealed their disagreement with me that Ballet is a masochistic profession. It definitely is for me. Apparently, others are aware of much less pain than I, and I suspect the way I drive myself through my pain barrier is by releasing sexual energy into it. Would my passion for dance alter if I had a fulfilled love life? Or will my obsession with dance be a barrier to personal fulfilment? Do I work harder than others, or is ballet simply more demanding on my body than on theirs? Perhaps in time I'll find the answers to these questions.

January 20th 1981

I spent a pleasant Christmas with relatives, though I missed my parents. On Boxing Day there was the premiere of the scarecrow ballet and the contemporary one *Von Vier Kanten Gezien*. I savoured every delicious moment of performing the organic movements of the latter and acquainted the soles of my feet with the performance floor.

Ten days break over the New Year enabled me to go home. My father drove me back to Holland helping me to transport possessions from London in his car. He stayed a week and with his good taste and expertise my room was transformed into a lovely home.

I'm learning the principal role in *Cyclus* by Peter Sawtell. It's a ballet for one woman and four men who represent male characters at different stages in her life from childhood to death. The central role is dramatic and I'm so happy to be involved with it. I have been promised performances. Again the programme planning has been disappointing and the ballets in which I have featured parts have been removed from the schedule. This is something to do with artistic decisions about which ballets are suitable for children's performances. Many of our shows take place during the day for very young audiences. This often involves getting up at 6am to catch a bus from Scapino's studios at 7.30am. There are also evening performances for adult audiences. It feels like jet lag sometimes with constant changes to the daily schedule. Performances can start at any time from 10.30am to 8pm.

February 5th 1981
Something very special happened today. The girl who is first cast in *Cyclus* was sick and I took her place in the rehearsal. We ran the fifteen-minute piece and at the end, and to my surprise and delight, my colleagues who were watching burst into spontaneous applause. This ballet does not stretch me but gives me a chance to pull my experience together into a compact mould. It certainly is a pleasure to dance.

February 8th 1981
I was again applauded at the rehearsal of *Cyclus* today. It gives me such a warm feeling when my dancing is respected and appreciated by my colleagues.

Rehearsals have started for a ballet by the ballet master, Fernand Daudey, to music by Dvorak. It is a classical piece on pointe and I'm to have the leading role in it. It will be good for us to work on as it demands stamina and is fairly difficult technically.

I find I'm getting very tired now, especially as I'm busier in the performances. My free time tends to be spent spaced out in front of the television. There is not much time or energy left over to go out, but when I do, one of my favourite haunts is Amsterdam's main library. It has a pleasant coffee shop where one can sit and read, and I am raiding the music section which has a large collection of classical records and cassettes.

Thinking about the summer holidays I've decided to book a ten-day trip to Russia, a country I've long dreamed of visiting. I'm determined to enjoy my holiday this summer as I don't feel I've had a proper break for three years.

February 23rd 1981

Yesterday we performed at a new theatre in Rotterdam. We had been to a new theatre in another part of this town about a month ago and I found it most disconcerting that the two buildings are like twins. The design is the same, and the layout of the entire theatre is identical. It was spooky.

February 26th 1981

On tour in Northern Holland, we spend a couple of nights in a luxury motel. As I am only involved in one performance I have the rest of the time to sight see, wander around the town and even go to the zoo; though I feel sorry for the animals in the snow. I am looking forward to a long weekend at home in London soon.

March 3rd 1981

Thinking too much again ...

I don't have any major problems. On the surface life looks settled, secure and organised. Maybe that's the problem. I've no enormous battle to fight; just the normal daily ones of doing my work well, maintaining my weight, living my life. I've come to the conclusion that thinking too much is very dangerous for me, but whatever artful means I find to divert myself, I can't help feeling. The things I feel find their way into my subconscious, if I don't let them into my conscious thought. I'm constantly searching for a way to live my life, which is directly reflected in my constant attempts at dieting. Eating dulls the senses I find. Maybe that's why I'm tempted to over indulge and binge. It wouldn't matter if my career wasn't so dependent on my shape and physical condition.

What am I running away from when I try to dull my feelings? All sorts of things: my little dissatisfactions seem so trivial I'm ashamed to admit them considering the positive aspects of my life. One alarming philosophy I run into every so often is the old question - why? What is the point of it all? Mostly my life has been filled with purpose but sometimes I question my choice of a dancing career. I ask myself, is all the agony and pain I am constantly torturing myself with worth it? It's very tempting to try to find an easy way out and say it is not worth it. But life is full of commitments that one has to make and none are easy to stick to. Few commitments involve the physicality of ballet and I seem to have both a good and a bad deal in my talent. The parts which come naturally: the grace, musicality, artistry, performing charisma, these things help. But the fact that I have to work so hard on my stupid thighs and bum is quite literally "a pain in the arse"!

Dancing is an escape from the reality of life for me, and the realities of life are an escape from the gruelling profession. I love Scapino for its relaxed working environment, and variable schedule. I admit how positive and satisfying life is here. Yet I am starved for more artistic stimulation.

I am thankful for the sculpting which gives me artistic pleasure and I'm getting commissions from dancers to make figurines for them. I must rest. I must learn to cope with being tired...

March 7th 1981

Between performances today I broke in a new pair of pointe shoes, first hammering them and then working them in by practising. It was most rewarding as I ended up working in a totally concentrated yet spontaneous way achieving a lot with little effort. I think it is called inspiration! All of a sudden I saw the light guiding me out the dark abyss of self criticism and hate. Instead of regarding my body as an imperfect instrument that gives me pain and never achieves the ideals of perfection I set it, I saw it as a toy to play with and discover just what its possibilities really are. Fatigue is my big enemy. Dancing is such a physical thing it is so easy to lose confidence when my body hurts and feels out of control. My little bit of inspired activity today reminded me that it is worth the effort - for a little longer at least.

March 28th 1981

News that Dublin City Ballet has been disbanded confirms I made a wise decision in coming to Amsterdam. Had I stayed in Ireland I would be unemployed now; not a joyous thought.

My mother and I enjoyed her visit last week very much. She came with us on the bus to watch performances and was able to see her family here too.

Armando Navarro is choreographing a new ballet *Humoresque* to music by Dvorak. I have a central role in it. In one section I am chased around the stage in a flowing robe by a wind machine masquerading as a film camera. He has chosen my favourite Slavonic dance for this part and I am thrilled to have something specially choreographed for me to this music; a dream come true. The lyrical style suits me well.

Rehearsals of Matt Mattox's *Jazz Etudes* are in progress. It is a challenging piece and I'm thankful for all the jazz classes I attended in Ireland.

April 11th 1981

In desperation, because of injuries, they finally put me on in *Concerto Grosso*. My forward roll was messy, more of a sideways roll, which is a shame as I can do everything else well, but I seem to get away with it.

May 1st 1981

Today is "Queen's Day" in Holland. Celebrations in Amsterdam include an open market allowing anyone to sell anything. It is quite chaotic, the streets crowded with impromptu stalls, and children happily bringing out all their old toys and comics to sell for a few cents.

I have decided I must stop feeling inadequate because I do not have a boyfriend and learn to enjoy my own company more.

May 5th 1981

It is "Liberation Day". All the flags are out to celebrate the day the allies freed Holland from German occupation. The Dutch still remember how they suffered during the Second World War. I have found I must take care because I have a slight German accent when I speak Dutch, and people can be quite cool towards me if they suspect I am German.

May 16th 1981

My Dutch cousin drove me to Zaanse Schans this evening. It is a picturesque village with painted houses and windmills set in the middle of the countryside amongst grazing cattle. On our return to Amsterdam he decided we would surprise his friend Hein, who recently moved here from the country, and invite ourselves to coffee. Hein seemed pleased to see us. He was very hospitable and more open than when I met him before. He has a pleasant flat overlooking the rooftops and canals. It was an enjoyable evening and he offered me an open invitation to return. I thought this was rather nice.

It is good to hear that Janet Lewis has been able to reform her company in England and prospects are optimistic. My former flatmate in Ireland has a contract as ballet master in Gothenberg in Sweden. I am so pleased for him as I know this is what he wanted.

May 26th 1981

The last performance for this season is over. No-one cheered, put the flags up or opened a bottle of champagne. Everyone drifted through with a vague look in their eyes, too exhausted to show any emotion.

The final weeks of the season will consist of rehearsals in preparation for next season and a choreographic workshop in which I am not involved. Perhaps I shall make use of this excellent opportunity for the dancers to experiment with their own creative ideas sometime, but I am far too exhausted this year.

John Boorman has won a prize at the Cannes Film Festival for his film *Excalibur* and I am excited to think that I was in a prize-winning film. I can't wait to see it.

My flatmate and I have little contact as she has so many evening performances and sometimes is away on tour. When she is home, I am often working. She is progressing fast with the Dutch National Ballet and it seems that jealousy amongst her colleagues is robbing her of their friendship.

Regular visits from the five cats in the household are a welcome bonus in my life. It's so delightful to be visited by these furry friends without having the responsibility of looking after them all the time.

June 11th 1981
They say criminals return to the scene of the crime... and here I am in Düsseldorf again briefly visiting friends. I was struck immediately on arrival by how grey the place is. It is not improved by engineering work in progress to build an underground railway. Admittedly the town seemed almost bearable when the sun came out in a clear blue sky, and walking in the Hofgarten park was civilised compared to strolling through the tangle of hippies and punks in Amsterdam's Vondel Park. I still ask myself a hundred times over how on earth I survived three years here, remembering how often I dreaded going to work. Everything seems very distant, strange and foreign; any trace of familiarity has gone. It is peculiar to be like a stranger and yet instinctively know my way around the back streets. I never belonged here and I certainly do not now.

****

August 10th 1981
Ironically, the hardest part of settling into life in Amsterdam again is adjusting to the familiarity and not feeling out of my depth like I used to in Düsseldorf. It is strange to feel that I do almost belong as I have a happy life here, even though I miss home and my parents.

The performance schedule looks promising and I expect to be working very hard. *Coppélia* Act Two will be in our repertoire but soloists from the big group are cast to dance Swanhilda. I asked Armando why this is as I'd been promised the leading roles with Scapino 10, and this was my motivation to stay a second season. He appeared to have forgotten this. I

71

offered to be ready to step in if anyone got injured; after all I have danced it before, even if the production was different.

I feel refreshed after a marvellous holiday, spending a lot of time with my parents at home and in Switzerland, and visiting Russia. The ten-day trip to Moscow and Leningrad had a profound effect on me and the way I see things.

I was fascinated by everything in the Soviet Union. It was all so different from anything I had experienced before. The modern buildings were different, very concrete and functional. The people were different with their Slavic features and dowdy clothes. I had tried to choose the simplest outfits I possessed from my wardrobe, but I was still clearly a westerner and was constantly being offered a price for my clothes, sunglasses, even my hair clips. I could have made a fortune in rubbles and returned home naked!

I took advantage of the excursions arranged for us by our Soviet travel agent, Intourist, and duly saw all the important monuments and museums. I was touched by the paintings depicting the hard life of the people coping with their climate, especially the long dark winters. Tour guides were keen to make us aware of their history and recent industrial achievements. Indeed it was all most impressive.

The Russian underground is an experience in itself with its endless escalators plunging deep below ground level into a large, elegant, spotlessly clean maze of tunnels. No-one would dream of dropping litter or writing graffiti here. I had learned some Russian and understood the alphabet which enabled me to wander around on my own. This would be virtually impossible without being able to decipher the symbols of the alphabet. I only regretted my Russian was not up to having proper conversations. However, I did manage to buy a ticket to a ballet performance by a provincial company at the Conservatorium theatre in Leningrad next to the Kirov. Of course, I was disappointed that the Kirov was shut, and it was not possible to go to the Bolshoi in Moscow either. I saw *The Fountain of Bakhchisarai*, a truly Russian ballet. I was just so thrilled to see Russian dancers on a Russian stage, I had tears rolling down my cheeks. The whole trip was rather dramatic for me, perhaps because it was something I had dreamed of for a long time.

The things which made the greatest impression on me were the lack of advertising, except for the giant red political murals, and the lack of variety in the shops. I realised that in the West I am constantly bombarded by advertising, which in fact is a source of entertainment and diversion from my inner thoughts. In Russia I saw things more clearly, including myself, because there were not these distractions. I also felt disgusted by the amount of choice we are given in the West, where supermarkets are lined with endless rows of any make of any product. In Russia, coffee is coffee, tea is tea, and you can be thankful if there is any on the shelves. Rather than feeling sorry for the Russians, I found myself questioning the morality of my own lifestyle. I felt embarrassed returning to my local Albert Heijn supermarket by the range of choice for anything on my shopping list.

On the way back to Amsterdam we had to change planes in Stockholm. I sent my parents a postcard from Arlanda Airport, in transit in a city I had barely heard of. It was a strange feeling because although Stockholm is a European capital, it seems as remote to me as the African jungle.

August 13th 1981

The most peculiar thing has happened. This afternoon, Fernand, who choreographed the Dvorak ballet and is rehearsing it, announced that he was dissatisfied with the casting and another girl was to learn my part. I just could not believe it, especially as the other girl is very rounded and not a strong classical dancer. After the rehearsal I went to talk to him. The girl who originally danced the principal role was exceptionally tall and he used this in the choreography. As I do not have any outstanding features, he decided to use a large busted girl instead. He also wants a harder approach in the characterisation, and finds I am too soft and feminine. I feel this is unfair as I have only been taught the steps and given no indication about interpretation. My natural instincts were apparently the wrong ones. I told him I would surprise him and he agreed to let me continue working on the part at the side. I am to learn the place of the girl replacing me, and she has no solos. I was tempted to complain more, and remind him that I signed another contract in the belief that I would be dancing principal roles. But I do respect a choreographer's opinion of his work. So I shall accept the situation and do my best to prove him wrong.

Jazz Etudes is not scheduled to be performed despite the weeks of rehearsals before the summer holiday. So *Humoresque* is the most interesting piece for me at the moment. I hope this is not taken away as well.

August 16th 1981

I notice a change in myself this season. For the first time in my life I enjoy working at my dancing for the sake of the work. I have always been concerned with emotions before: love of dancing, or ambition. But now I work hard because it gives me satisfaction to work positively at something, and pride in a doing a good job. Perhaps at last I am starting to be

73

"professional". This does not affect my love of my Art or my desire to achieve success, but it ensures that whatever happens I shall enjoy the simple fulfilment of work. Also, I find I get on much better with everyone this year. I suppose I am more relaxed and less intense on trying to make a good impression.

Another novelty this year is the introduction of a forty-five minute lunch break. It really helps having time to eat and digest. It also helps psychologically to pace oneself through the day.

August 17th 1981

Fernand is stuck with me after all! The girl he put in my place has injured herself. It doesn't surprise me, I know her pointe work is weak.

August 24th 1981

Fernand had not said a word to me about his ballet until this afternoon when, to my delighted amazement, he complimented me on it and said that I had proved myself to him. I don't know why I so often have to battle to prove myself to people, but it seems a regular pattern in my life.

I saw *Excalibur* for the third time, finally spotting myself during the two seconds I appear on the screen. I like the film very much, there is a strong, magical atmosphere enhanced by powerful music.

September 10th 1981

Yesterday during a walk through the cobbled streets and canals of central Amsterdam, I took Hein up on his invitation to drop by. He gave me a coffee and invited me to spend the day on the beach with him today. We went to Zandvoort, the nearest beach to Amsterdam. It's a rather flat boring beach, just sand and crowds of people. However, it was a warm, sunny day and the sea air made a welcome break from town. We basked in the sun and paddled in the sea. A tall, lanky, bearded Dutchman, Hein is a quiet person. He is an environmental architect, ten years my senior, and reads a lot. He speaks fluent English so again I am not destined to improve my Dutch. It's so embarrassing to speak bad Dutch to Dutch people who speak perfect English.

September 15th 1981

Fernand has started a new ballet, *Colombine*, to be performed in schools. There are two casts and I share the title role. It is the story of Colombine who gets lost in the woods, turned into a frog by the witch, and saved by Harlequin and Pierrot at the end. I am on pointe, apart from when I become a frog and have to dance in flippers - another new experience! The part involves a lot of acting which I enjoy. Fernand is very enthusiastic about his new ballet and it is inspiring work.

September 28th 1981

Hein's dinner invitation on Saturday was a quiet, pleasant one, and a perfect distraction from my nerves for the following day's premiere of *Humoresque*. The performance went smoothly despite my anxieties. I was in the unusual situation of feeling over rehearsed, and this can be as scary as being under rehearsed. With over rehearsal there is no excuse to make any mistakes. After six months working on this piece it's a relief to perform it at last. It was so lovely that my Dutch cousin, Emma and her husband came to see me dance. At last I can invite friends to see shows and know they will see me: no sheets or obscurity in the back row. Armando seemed well pleased with his creation.

October 5th 1981

I have felt somewhat deflated since the premiere, but work continues as normal. Reviews have been good, also praising my dancing. I have received positive feedback from colleagues and the management too. As I am more exposed in the parts I dance this season, I have more opportunity to present my qualities.

Fate is giving me my chance to prove myself as Swanhilda here, due to another's injury yet again. I shall dance it next week. Taking responsibility to learn the role on my own (it differs from the production in Ireland) has been appreciated by the direction. As rehearsal time is limited I practise whenever I can.

October 15th 1981

It was so lovely to be Swanhilda again, like coming home. It felt comfortable. I was congratulated by fellow dancers and the direction. This was particularly enjoyable because my father is visiting and was able to see the performance. He travelled to the theatre in Drachten on his motorbike and I returned with him. It was a memorable ride, completely different from my role as a ballerina in the theatre that afternoon, but equally thrilling. The silver clouds dancing before a yellow sky predicting the imminent storm, as we sped on our way back to Amsterdam, could have been the set for a Wagner opera.

Hein came to dinner and met my father. He brought me a present of clay for my sculptures, which was very thoughtful. We are becoming friends, but not in a romantic way, though I feel there is affection between us. Neither of us is concerned with impressing the other. We say what we think, do as we feel honestly and with consideration, but without ulterior motives. One way and another with my work, social life flourishing and sculpture commissions, my life is fully occupied right now; there are not enough hours in the day to do everything.

November 21st 1981

We are in the midst of a heavy touring schedule. The variety of places we visit is interesting. For example, Ahlen is in Germany. Surprisingly, it still upsets me a little to be in Germany. The audience was completely different from the Dutch public. People were much more reserved in Ahlen suppressing their laughter in the humorous sections but applauding warmly at every opportunity. Whereas Dutch audiences will laugh loudly and clap less. Maastricht a few days later, on the other hand, is South near the border with Belgium. It is a cosy town, full of traditional Flemish character.

Hein and I have been getting to know each other better. He has asked me to accompany him on a visit to his sister, her husband and their newly born "monster", as he calls his nephew, in Gothenburg in Sweden. I will be able to see my former flatmate from Ireland who is ballet master with the company there.

December 6th 1981

Things are heating up with Hein. After two and half years of being single, it is such a relief and pleasure to finally have a boyfriend again. He found it hard to believe that I had been alone for so long. I am looking forward to our trip together. Hein is an easy-going, calm companion and it will be the first time I go on holiday with a boyfriend.

December 11th 1981

I had a rather confusing review of my work with Armando. He told me that I have not improved in my role of Swanhilda in *Coppélia* since I started doing it. He claimed to be dissatisfied with how I am performing it, but he would not go into details about what is wrong or how I can improve. He then went on to say that generally the direction are pleased with my work, and offered me a substantial pay rise. I asked the ballet staff what is wrong with my dancing as Swanhilda and they could not say; further confusion. Perhaps Armando is challenging me to achieve more.

December 20th 1981

A very special Christmas present arrived for me when my parents were dropped from heaven! They had been on holiday in Portugal and their plane returning to London was unable to land due to bad weather conditions. Eventually after some time circling, the only airport which would offer the plane a landing slot was Amsterdam's Schipol airport. The passengers were taken to a hotel and I went to see my parents. It really was an extraordinary sensation to suddenly have them there for a few hours.

Amsterdam is very pretty in the snow with Christmas decorations and people skating on the canals. The Dutch seem to enjoy the seasonal festivities and indulge in decorative chocolate Christmas trees and Santa Claus figures.

January 14th 1982

Once again, I spent Christmas with relatives. I didn't eat very much because I had to dance Swanhilda on Boxing Day.

As planned, during our break I went to Sweden which looked like fairyland under thick snow. However, I was not impressed by Gothenberg, finding it a dull town. I decided I had seen enough of Sweden, it is a country I need not return to.

Hein was a good companion and accompanied me to see a ballet performance and a rehearsal. It was great fun to see my flatmate from Dublin City Ballet again and interesting to observe the ballet company in Sweden. Copenhagen caught my fantasy much more than Gothenberg. I explored the town during a three hour wait to change trains there on my way to meet Hein in Sweden, and promised myself to return one day.

A cast list has gone up for this month's performances and I shall be dancing Swanhilda a lot; apparently I have improved now. I shall be very busy. I am lucky that Hein is patient and undemanding. He is always relaxing company; in fact I tend to spend most of Sundays sleeping and he accepts this. It is just my luck that now I have a boyfriend at last, I have little time to appreciate him.

My flatmate complains how little work she has at present with the Dutch National Ballet. I sympathise with her frustration and understand her impatience. She has been promised more work but her height limits the parts she can be cast for despite her exceptional talent. I am grateful to be so busy.

January 30th 1982

Life goes on with endless performances, classes and rehearsals. My spare time is given to a lot of sleeping, some socialising with Hein and friends, and occasional outings to the theatre and cinema.

School demonstrations make a welcome break from the tensions of performances and rehearsals. They are never boring because every audience is so different and there is a direct contact with the children. Sometimes it's quite a challenge to capture their interest and concentration. As we do not get a class on demonstration days, I usually take a tape along to accompany my warm up, and my colleagues sometimes join me. I find it important to maintain self-discipline during these times, otherwise my technique suffers.

February 5th 1982

By the end of a full week of demonstrations (two a day plus travelling) I start to feel shattered. If the pale faces in the canteen waiting for the vans at 7.30am each morning are anything to judge by, I am not the only one. It will be almost a relief to get back to the familiarity of class and five hours of rehearsal.

February 11th 1982

It's bliss to know that I don't have another morning performance for the rest of this month. I can be as grumpy as I like in the mornings now! It can be tough having to be bright and cheerful when I am barely awake.

I was let off rehearsals this afternoon so I have come home to rest. I've made a sculpture and now I'll watch television and go to bed early. My body feels shattered. It is numb from exhaustion: at least it has passed the pain level. I had a lot of pain last week and at the beginning of this week, from pushing my muscles to their limits.

February 25th 1982

I feel exhausted. Occasionally, my energy picks up, but mostly I feel tired, depressed and suffer extreme muscle soreness. When I am still I can escape the aching muscles, but they scream at me when I move. Balletic movements are particularly painful when my body wants to rest and not to dance. I went to the doctor who gave me a tonic and suggested I take a holiday. Not much chance of that unfortunately. It can't be much fun for Hein having me as a girlfriend. My favourite pastime is to curl up and go to sleep.

March 4th 1982

A lot of the recent fatigue is explained by the loss of a few drops of blood. This is the nearest thing to a reminder of my womanhood that I've had in a year, and that was a very light period too. I haven't had a proper monthly flow since my weight dropped below 51 kilos. I seem to pass through cycles, however, as I am aware of mood swings and fluctuations in energy.

March 14th 1982

I'm beginning to accept that I shall be in a state of exhaustion till the end of season. It was suggested to me by a friend (not a dancer) that my work must keep me very fit. I had to shatter his illusions and tell him that I feel ill most of the time. I find it difficult to accept the pain. I still have a hard time accepting the toughness of the profession. By thinking of the pain as a challenge to deal with, I manage to keep going. I usually enjoy performances once I have warmed up my tired body, broken into a sweat and the adrenalin kicks in.

March 20th 1982

The marathon of performances all over Holland continues. I was exceptionally tired for one in Veghel a couple of days ago and resented having to do the Cancan before Swanhilda. The audience seemed sleepy during the first half of the show so I resolved to wake them up after the interval with *Coppélia*. My technique was shaky but I gave it all I had, and in the end there was warm applause and people stood up to show their appreciation. We came across a review in a local paper the following day. It was especially complimentary about my dancing as Swanhilda. It claimed that *Coppélia* was the highlight of the evening, and my dancing was "inspiring". (*Brabants Dagblad* 17/03/1982)

Receiving public recognition of my efforts helps ease my conscience about putting work before the relationship with Hein. It must be hard for him to understand that getting enough sleep and preparing for the next performance is more important than being with him. After all, my dancing is my livelihood.

Working with Scapino is never boring. We dance in the tiniest and the largest venues: in school halls, large sports halls, slick modern theatres and characterful old theatres. Recently we were in an unusually small space. We were literally on top of the audience and a little girl offered me a sweet in the middle of the performance! But it is often in these smaller, obscurer venues where the public is most appreciative.

March 23rd 1982

I'm not the only one who is tired. Unfortunately, some of my colleagues don't seem to take their work as seriously as I do and they allow their boredom to show onstage. A compensation for my determination to maintain professionalism was praise from the ballet mistress in front of the other dancers. The positive aspect is that my anger gives me energy which helps to keep me going.

My flatmate is getting more work now and I saw her dance the principal role in George Balanchine's *Theme and Variations*. It is fiendishly difficult but she makes it look easy and spontaneous.

News from home tells me that my father is having serious problems with his bad back. I wish I could make the pain less for him. It's a strain for my mother as well, and there's nothing constructive I can do to help from here.

April 1st 1982

There is an anti bosom blitz at Scapino! Four girls were told to lose weight, two more were taken out of *Humoresque*, and then after over thirty performances of the ballet in white lycra leotards and skirts, we were all given bras to wear. It certainly took them long enough to decide the costumes were unflattering to female torsos. There is never a dull moment! Lucky for me, I am practically flat chested.

April 22nd 1982

My back went into a spasm of knots after an unusually heavy rehearsal a few days ago. I burst into floods of tears from the pain in the studio and everyone was most kind and sympathetic. I was replaced in the scarecrow ballet so I can try to pull myself together for *Coppélia* next week. I'm determined not to give in, even though there are times I almost wish I would be injured just so that I could have a break. Rest and massage seem to be curing the back spasm.

April 29th 1982

I fell onstage today. People were tired and making mistakes, and by contrast I was full of energy. I must have been over confident because I tripped in a fast section towards the end. I don't know what happened. Suddenly I was aware that I had fallen and like lightening I was on my feet again smiling as though nothing had happened. I didn't know that I can move so fast! Afterwards the ballet master enquired if I was alright, and I appreciated his consideration, quite prepared to be ticked off for the mishap.

May 5th 1982

I celebrated my 41st performance in this production of *Coppélia*. The direction seems well pleased with my work, but the most enthusiastic compliment came from the firemen watching in the wings. Apparently, they thought I was "fantastic". I wonder if they were referring to my performance onstage or to the one in the wings when I changed costumes!

We are rehearsing a new ballet by Patricia Kapp to music by Poulenc about Barbar the Elephant to be premiered at the Holland Festival in June. I am the rich lady who befriends Barbar and the only member of the cast to dance on pointe. Thus I dance a pas de deux with an elephant - wonders will never cease!

May 9th 1982

After taking a couple of days off, I returned to work today. I'm in an exhausted trance. My body seems numb and I have difficulty in feeling and controlling my muscles. There is no physical energy. The power of the mind is amazing and somehow I go through the motions.

It's months since I last saw my relatives in Holland. They are offended that I have not visited them recently. It must be hard for them to appreciate how busy I've been, often working through two weeks with shows on Sundays. When I work so hard and travel all the time, I really just want to stay peacefully at home on free days. Sometimes I sleep most of the day anyway. Sometimes I see Hein, but there is lethargy in the relationship and often I prefer solitude. Being alone is pleasant as it's warm and sunny and I can take advantage of my beautiful balcony. Also there is always someone in the house preventing me from feeling completely isolated.

May 29th 1982

Despite my exhaustion, the last *Coppélia* of the season was tremendous fun. We played traditional last performance tricks. Swanhilda's friends tried to catch me out with various subtle changes in the choreography and I had to be super alert to respond within the context of the story. I also made some adjustments, for instance at the end of the Spanish variation I usually throw the rose I have been dancing with to Dr Coppelius. Today I made a gesture as if to throw it, but kept it so he looked silly trying to catch nothing as he anticipated my throw. It was all good fun.

June 3rd 1982

Since my heaviest performances are over for this season, I have a strong instinct that I must do auditions next year. I must give myself the chance to dance somewhere else and be stimulated by a different repertoire before I become stale here. I also realise that the relationship with Hein was a pleasant affair, but it's not going anywhere. I experience a sense of loss about this, loss of hope rather than anything tangible. We are not really compatible, and he can be so reserved sometimes; I don't know how to reach him. He makes no effort to keep us together.

The premiere of *Barbar* was a great success. The audience had to be stopped from clapping eventually because the dancers in the roles of Barbar and his sweetheart were busy getting out of their stifling elephant costumes and couldn't take any more calls. I enjoy making myself up as an old lady and use talcum powder to grey my hair.

June 15th 1982

I've been advised to rest for a few days by a doctor. My legs were throbbing all weekend and I'm simply too tired to dance. I've also been prescribed tablets for my blood pressure which is very low. Now I have no more performances, my body has gone on strike.

June 17th 1982

I've been called back from my sick bed to do a demonstration. Everyone is sick or injured and if I can't do it, they will have to cancel it. So I'll do it.

July 2nd 1982

As the season draws to a close, I am learning a solo role in Fernand's ballet *Pulcinella* for next season. My part is on pointe and is nice as it requires acting as well. The cast is mixed from the two groups of the company which will be merging next year into one large group.

My body is aching less, but susceptible to minor injuries, so I have to be careful not to hurt myself. It's still difficult for me to relax and unwind as my work demands so much energy from me.

****

August 24th 1982

After a relaxing holiday in London and Switzerland, I arrived back in Amsterdam. The new season, which is Scapino's 38th in existence, has started. Apparently the financial situation is insecure. We have been instructed to put 100% energy into our work to produce the best possible performances and prove our worth, to ensure financial support from the government. I'd like to think I always do… Otherwise everything is back to normal with the hectic routine of classes and rehearsals.

September 3rd 1982

An old friend whom I have not seen for years but have kept in vague contact with is staying with me for a few days. She is enjoying Amsterdam and I am enjoying her company which helps compensate for my inevitable homesickness after a holiday.

We are working very hard with the introduction of evening rehearsals. Working hours are 10am -5pm and 8 - 10pm. It is really heavy when one finds oneself involved in all the rehearsals. Sometimes I find I should be in two studios at the same time.

The feeling that I must leave is growing. I absolutely need the stimulation of a new working environment. I would almost prefer to stop dancing than to stay here a fourth year.

September 20th 1982

There is a general feeling of tension at Scapino as we waste endless hours in long, drawn out rehearsals. If people worked efficiently, less time would be needed for rehearsals. But since the management decided we should work longer hours, the work expands to fill the time, unnecessarily in my opinion. I feel tired and depressed all the time.

Several of my colleagues have asked me recently if I eat properly as I look so pale. They suspect me of dieting too much, perhaps with reason, but I have to keep as thin as possible to stop my hips from becoming large and out of proportion with my narrow shoulders. It occurs to me that because I take my work seriously, I feel responsible for my physical imperfections. I blame myself for the way nature made me and I cannot be at peace with myself unless I know I am being disciplined in my eating habits. I hate myself if my willpower slackens just a little. The only way I can accept my body is if I know I am doing the best I can to keep it as sleek as possible without actually starving. The problem is that I do not have my full energy capacity when my weight is low and I am continually cheating myself of the calories it needs to function. Thus I live in a state of permanent fatigue.

October 10th 1982

Three dancers have left the company since August, all of them to give up dancing. It is not a good situation for the company.

A friend who left last year is doing the Professional Dancer's Teaching Course at the Royal Academy of Dance in London and told me all about it when he was back in Holland recently. It sounds a very stimulating and interesting course. I've been following its progress since it started a few years ago. My former teacher at the Royal Ballet School, Julia Farron, is the director and I would love to work with her again. If I am unable to get another dancing job, I shall try to do this course. Apparently, it is hard physical work and I should be able to stay in shape, even improve my technique, so I could dance again afterwards if I wanted to. I have always known that I shall teach when I stop dancing so, sooner or later, I intend doing this course and qualifying as a ballet teacher.

My father is visiting and giving me much needed moral support as well as his wonderful company.

October 15th 1982

There have been riots in Amsterdam again as police remove squatters from a house at the top of our road. A burned out tram was dragged down the track and passed our front door looking reminiscent of Beirut. I find it all most unnerving and will be glad when it is over.

October 20th 1982

My father left this morning after an usually long visit of three and a half weeks. We have such a beautiful relationship, and as I mature, we meet on a spiritual level as friends, as well as father and daughter. I wrote a poem to help me get through a moment of wrenching pain.

To my Father
The pain of parting
Which tears my soul inside
One of life's many sufferings
To have to say goodbye

Each farewell
Leaves another hole
And yet the memories
Feed the soul

To appreciate togetherness
The comfort so secure
It is necessary to be alone
To know a love so pure

October 23rd 1982

It was fun to take the night train to Basle arriving in Switzerland at six in the morning. Everything is so clean and organised and curiously familiar, reminding me of happy summer holidays. I saw Swiss chocolate everywhere I looked, tempting me. "Eat me!"

I auditioned once again for Heinz Spoerli in the underground studios of the theatre, though I doubt if he remembered me. He rejected me on the grounds that I am too tall and not what he is looking for. I felt a little disheartened, but I'm not convinced this would be a good place for me. I do not like the prison-like windowless studios, and all that chocolate just might tempt me to become fat again. There must be something waiting for me, somewhere ...

October 29th 1982

I have just received yet another letter from my mother begging me to audition for the Dutch National Ballet. I know my insecure situation worries her and she would like me to stay in Holland. I have enjoyed living here but now I have itchy feet and I'm desperate for a new challenge. I don't think I would be accepted into the Dutch National, and even if I was, I would almost certainly have very little work in the beginning and be bored. I don't know if I could cope with that or the intense competitive atmosphere there. Besides, my skeleton will be the wrong shape for the director, Rudi van Dantzig, no matter how skinny I am. My mother does not understand this.

October 30th 1982

This week has been a touring one and we have travelled to a different place every day. I enjoy my performance schedule this year because I always have featured parts as a soloist, but as some ballets are double cast I get rests and do not feel as frantic as last year. Thus, I also have more free time to look around the places we visit and some towns are now quite familiar.

A piece by Nils Christie had been premiered. It was commissioned by the Board of Energy with specially composed music which is one of its best features. A very large sum of money was provided for the production and the first performance was a private one for the employees and their families. In a speech given beforehand it was proudly announced that there would be fifty public performances and one hundred school ones of *Op is Op* (the new ballet) this season. Backstage, faces paled at the prospect. Some parts are nice to dance, but not all of them. It is a ballet for the audience rather than the dancers with lots of changes of props and costumes, and special effects. I do not mind at all not being in it.

November 4th 1982

My flatmate is sulking because she has to rehearse till six every evening with performances afterwards with Dutch National Ballet. Nederlans Dans Theatre also works very long hours. There is no union here to protect the dancers as in many other countries. They are mad in this country!

November 10th 1982

I've had a new idea regarding auditions. After studying a map to see where I could go, avoiding Germany, Scandinavia seems a possibility and I am going to write to the companies there with a view to a soloist contract. I am also contacting Festival Ballet and Northern Ballet at home, and Ballet van Vlaanderen in Antwerp.

A studio, aptly named "Try-out", has opened in Amsterdam providing open classes for professional dancers. It is the first of its kind here as far as I know, and is very useful and stimulating for dancers. The classes are in the evenings so, when I have time and energy, I go there. Just like attending open classes in London, I always meet people I know and it's as much a social outing as a working one.

November 25th 1982

A visit to an old friend from the Royal Ballet School, who now dances in Frankfurt, refreshed and inspired me. It was great fun to see each other again after seven years, though I am sorry she is having problems. She is very lonely as she is missing her family, and has accepted to dance in the corps de ballet again after giving up her senior soloist position in her previous company. She has been promised opportunities there, which was the reason she took the job, but these are slow to materialise.

I was introduced to Egon Madsen who left Stuttgart Ballet to become director in Frankfurt, and watched him rehearsing his wife Lucia Isenring in a new ballet he is making. She is a beautiful dancer, a real "ballerina" in physique, temperament and presence and I loved watching her. Overall the standard of the dancers is high. At last I was able to be in Germany without feeling oppressed by grey memories of Düsseldorf. Frankfurt has a cosmopolitan feel to it which I like.

November 27th 1982

Fate works in curious ways; I received a letter from Scapino today offering me another contract and a small rise in salary, and I also received a letter from Stockholm offering me an audition for a corps de ballet position in the Royal Swedish Ballet. This is the only positive reply I have had; all the other companies are either full up or not taking foreign dancers.

December 1st 1982

Much to my mother's dismay, I have resigned from Scapino Ballet. Armando is looking pale as a lot of people are leaving this year, including many of his most valued dancers. My colleagues are surprised by my decision as I now have a comfortable, respected position in the company.

I am planning to audition in Stockholm during the winter break as well as in London for Festival Ballet. I have a strong instinct drawing me to Stockholm despite my negative impressions of Sweden last winter. My mouth waters when I read about the repertoire of the Royal Swedish Ballet: all the big classical ballets, plus ballets by MacMillan, Balanchine, Cranko, Kylian, Tudor … the list is endless. My only worries are being so far from home, and the cold winters. Also, I would have to accept dancing in the corps de ballet again. But it could be worth the risk to take a step backwards for the sake of the experience.

December 15th 1982

My mother's visit was less pleasurable than usual. She is very worried about my decision to leave Scapino and the insecurities and uncertainties of the future. I understand her feelings but find it difficult to accept that she cannot be more supportive. I try to share my enthusiasm with her about a new venture, and end up being dragged down by her pessimism.

December 19th 1982

I had an enjoyable and interesting evening at a colleague's birthday party this evening. There were several dancers from the Dutch National Ballet there. In my conversations with some of them, satisfaction levels varied. I was reminded that not all dancers are used all the time, and often they have to wait their turn for a chance to dance something interesting. One commented on the injustices in casting which she has witnessed throughout her long career and cannot understand. It all confirmed for me that I am making the right decision not to pursue this company despite my mother's insistence that I should. I know I'll have to wait for opportunities in a new company, but if I am in a new city I can distract myself and explore whilst I'm waiting.

December 28th 1982

I experienced an immense feeling of adventure after this evening's performance, the last before our winter break. The theatre was in Den Helder on the northern tip of the peninsular which is the province of North Holland, and the strong smell of sea salt in the air seemed like a premonition of some sort.

January 3rd 1983

In London for New Year, I took a class with Festival Ballet on the stage of the Festival Hall where they are   currently performing. John Field, the director, came to watch me. He told me he will not know what vacancies there will be until April. He seemed interested in me, but warned me that there are many strong dancers around looking for work and I shouldn't wait for Festival Ballet if I have the chance of a job elsewhere.

January 6th 1983

Yesterday I returned to Amsterdam and bought a cheap standby flight to Stockholm at Schipol airport. I did class at Try-out studios with a weird feeling of floating somewhere over Europe.

My alarm woke me at the uncivilised hour of 6am. I jumped out of bed to be ready in time for the taxi I had ordered. I arrived at the airport in good time and proceeded to check in. I went to the bank counter to cash a cheque in Swedish kronor and it was then that the cashier noticed that my cheque guarantee card had expired at the end of December 1982, and she refused to draw money on it. If I could wait till bank opening hours my branch could be contacted to authorise a transaction, but by then I would have missed my flight and my ticket could not be changed. In all the rush it just had not occurred to me that it was time to renew my cheque card. Luckily, I had sufficient cash for my needs, but my heart rose to my throat as I realised that I had bought a one way ticket leaving myself an option to return by train. I saw all my carefully considered plans crumble away as I imagined trying to buy my return ticket in Sweden with an expired cheque card.

Panic is unusual for me, but I was vulnerable as I was still half asleep, nervous about the whole trip, and had not eaten breakfast yet. I was sent to an information desk where I tried to explain my problem, but I was already feeling lightheaded and when I fainted against the desk and fell to the floor, the man behind the desk did not take me seriously. I was so shocked at having overlooked this detail after all the things I've had to organise recently, and then I was frustrated with myself for passing out. It was disconcerting afterwards to realise that no-one made any attempt to help me.

Precious time was lost and when I had pulled myself together again, I returned to the flight reservations desk where I had bought my outbound flight. Everyone seemed too busy and my honesty about the cheque card only prejudiced them against helping me. So, in desperation, I found another reservations area and emphasising the need for haste because my plane was due to leave in 30 minutes, I secured a return flight from Stockholm, and just like yesterday when I booked my outgoing flight, the lady also forgot that it is 1983. Phew! Feeling very shaky, I boarded the flight just as the doors were being closed and set off for Stockholm.

It was strange to arrive in Sweden as I am familiar with it from my stay here last winter, when I thought I would never return! The countryside is the same, undulating forests, and Stockholm is similar to Gothenberg but on a much grander scale. It strikes me as a beautiful city with elegant buildings and views across the islands on which it is built.

I took a bus into town which is 45 kilometres from the airport, and then an underground train to a hostel where I'd reserved a bed. I'm in a room with four bunks but so far I'm the sole occupant. Relief swept over me when I finally arrived with a roof over my head and I dropped into bed and slept for an hour.

Anxious not to miss my chance to see the town I went out as soon as I woke and headed for the Opera House. It is an austere but grand old building. I walked around the town and spent a couple of hours in the museum of modern art where there is a very fine Chagall exhibition. Stockholm is very pretty at night, which begins around 3pm this time of year, with sparkling lights reflected across the water. There is no snow and apparently it is mild for January. I brought warm clothes expecting to freeze, and find I am too hot. Swedes seem to be tall and the men are very handsome. I am curious to see the ballet company. People have been very friendly and helpful.

January 7th 1983

When I turned up for class at the Opera House this morning and saw the studio, I almost turned around and gave up there and then because the studio has a raked floor! I gazed in and it looked like I was going to spend the whole time dancing on a ski slope. Fortunately, something forced me to stick with the plan, maybe the thought that if I'd come this far, I may as well get a class out of it.

Just as well I took on the challenge of the raked studio floor as I have been offered a contract! It is a corps de ballet one, there are no soloist vacancies, but nevertheless it is nice to feel wanted. If Stockholm were not so far from London I would not hesitate to accept. I spoke with the director, Gunilla Roempke, and was encouraged by the promise of a superb repertoire and generous holidays allowing me chances to go home. She invited me to see the performance of Frederick Ashton's *La Fille Mal Gardée* this evening. This gives me a chance to assess the company and what the offer of a contract here really means.

Backstage the Opera House is luxurious and a sneaked glimpse of the stage brought tears to my eyes; a "real" stage with proscenium arch and ornate tiered auditorium. There are few of these in either Holland or Germany. A less pleasant surprise was the steep slope of the raked stage, but it made sense that a studio had the same sloped floor for rehearsals.

I am aware that I would be very alone here, not only personally but also professionally, in a large group of eighty dancers. Self-discipline would be essential. But this could be an extremely valuable experience if I plan to teach later. I still have time to consider the offer, but fate has brought me here and perhaps it would be enriching for my development to dance here for a year and take advantage of everything Stockholm has to offer. I could spend a year of free days just sight seeing, visiting museums and watching videos. There is a fantastic video library at the theatre with a private viewing room. There is no shortage of things to do. I am sure my parents would enjoy a visit here too.

This afternoon I went up the Kaknäs Tower just outside of Stockholm. From the observation platform 130 meters high there is a stunning view of the city and surrounding forests. One is aware of being close to nature and the Swedes know how to enjoy this. I also notice an emphasis on family life, and this does seem an ideal place to raise children.

January 8th 1983

At Arlanda airport awaiting the last lap of the adventure, I feel dreadful! After all the tension and excitement I can't wait to curl up in my bed in Amsterdam.

When I saw the performance last night there was no more doubt in my mind about accepting the contract. The dancing was of a high level, everyone was full of energy and enthusiasm and the overall production was excellent; exactly the same production as the Royal Ballet in London. The more I see of the town the more it grows on me, and I was completely overwhelmed by the luscious Opera House foyer and auditorium.

It is a theatre of my dreams and there is a lump in my throat to think I will be dancing there.

I met an English chap in the company who I know from the Royal Ballet School. He told me he finds Stockholm boring and has too much free time. He doesn't like operas, museums and sight seeing, so hopefully I won't have that problem; for a year anyway.

January 11th 1983

At last I'm managing to calm down a little as the knot in my stomach unwinds. It's extraordinary how instinct took me to Sweden. I felt so out of control; floating along on the waves of destiny driven by an indefinable force. I'm still floating but brought nearer to earth by the sore buttock from the massive bruise I acquired when I fainted at the airport.

Getting back into rehearsals at Scapino I have a sore back again. What absolute bliss it will be to have a masseur next year in Stockholm. There is also a sauna in the Opera House basement. I simply don't believe my luck; I have found a goldmine. My colleagues are impressed with my new job and many are envious.

I went to a performance by Nederlans Dans Theater a couple of days ago here in Amsterdam, and I feel so happy to be able to hope that one day I may still have the chance of dancing in a ballet by Jiri Kylian as his work is in the Swedish repertoire.

January 18th 1983

My contract arrived today helping me to believe that it's all really going to happen. The prospect of having to finish my contract here and wait seven months before I can go there is disheartening. There is nothing new for me at Scapino, just endless repetition of the same performances and long bus rides. I feel restless and impatient to start my new life and am rapidly learning Swedish from a teach yourself course. The other blot on my happiness is that instead of being pleased for me, my mother is very suspicious. She wants to see a copy of the contract and is nagging me about things I shall need to organise. I suppose she is worried, but I've done this before, started in a new company in a new country, and I am twenty four; no longer a baby. I wish she'd have a bit more faith in me.

January 25th 1983

Strained muscles in my groin which might be an indirect result of the fall have given me a few days off. I am under the care of a physiotherapist and am happy to have more time to study Swedish and relax. I could do with a good back massage, and I could do with a cuddle.

February 3rd 1983

There is some hope for my aches and pains after all. My doctor has prescribed massage treatment, so my Dutch health insurance will pay for it. The knots in my back have been gradually becoming more regular so it is like magic to be able to organise some relief for it.

I am getting occasional cramps again, due to stress I suspect. I certainly feel very stressed coping with this transition period before I can start my new job. Another dancer has experienced similar cramps and suggested a homeopathic tranquilliser which seems to help. I know life in Sweden will not be easy and see this as an opportunity to build up my resilience.

February 10th 1983

I was most touched today when colleagues told me they will miss me when I go to Stockholm. It is wonderful to be valued as a person and not measured only by my achievements, which is what I tend to do to myself. The latter brings me little happiness as I never feel I am achieving enough. Most of all I am so aware of my shortcomings as a dancer and not very good at reminding myself of my strengths. This must be part of the burden of being an artist.

A novelty in my life is the acquisition of a walkman so I can listen to music with my headphones whenever and wherever I want. Bus rides are a pleasure now with a concert ringing in my ears. I don't know how I managed without it. I can also listen to my Swedish tapes. I am three quarters of the way through the three month course already. What shall I do when I've finished it?

February 20th 1983

My obsession with Swedish continues and I have completed the three month course in six weeks. My Swedish reading is on a level with my Dutch. I've put more energy into learning Swedish the last weeks than I put into learning Dutch over the last three years.

February 25th 1983

After a few days tour in Germany involving long bus rides, I decided to go to class at the Try-out studio when we returned this evening. When the teacher didn't turn up we were given the option of a refund or doing the class on our own with the pianist. Everyone looked vacant so I eagerly volunteered to set a class which people could do if they liked or change the exercises. Everyone agreed and in the end they all stayed for the entire hour and a half and did the exercises as I set them. It was marvellous. I simply showed similar combinations to the ones I give myself when I practise, set a tempo for the pianist and we all worked together. People seemed to enjoy themselves and thanked me enthusiastically afterwards. It was thrilling to discover this new aspect of myself, and I am sure I will enjoy teaching one day.

March 13th 1983

Life is hectic and ridiculously unpredictable. People are dropping like flies and programmes are changed several times before a performance takes place. One day I was dragged out of class and within fifteen minutes found myself onstage in Scapino's studio theatre dancing a part I hadn't done for six months.

At long last I met my American cousin, Steve, from Seattle. He is a pilot on long haul flights and flew to Amsterdam this weekend. The only time he had free to meet was early in the morning, so I invited him to breakfast. It was odd to greet the stranger at the front door who gave me a warm bear hug and then have so much to talk about together. His wife is Swedish and he has friends in Stockholm with whom he told me to get in touch. Apparently he flies to Stockholm quite often so I hope I shall see him there.

I have a proper monthly flow for the first time in ages. It's no wonder I've been feeling irritable and tired recently. Successful dieting has been impossible; it has been too difficult to fight the natural need of my body for food. The arrival of a period is a relief, though I have to shed two kilos.

Coping with my job is tough at the moment. I find I disagree with many of the company's policies, especially the academic and artistic ones. Some of the approaches to technique used here are contrary to my training at the Royal Ballet School. An example is the use of the foot, which I was taught to articulate through the bones with sensitivity in the sole. Here they insist on a rigidly held foot under the metatarsal arch even when there is weight on the foot. I have tried to do as I was told since I arrived, but am starting to rebel against the things I don't believe in. When I auditioned for Festival Ballet recently, John Field (the director) observed the stiffness in my footwork. He also commented on my tense neck and shoulders; another fault encouraged by contraction instead of lengthening of muscles. This is a general fault of Scapino where problems are solved by gripping muscles with brute force, rather than coaxing them with concentration. The emphasis is on strength rather than quality and control. There is also a lack of artistic subtlety. Perhaps I ignored these things which concern me now because I was ambitious and, in order to achieve my goals in the company, had to make compromises. Now I feel less involved in the company, working towards a new beginning, I see things in a different light. I have tried to express my feelings on these matters with the ballet staff but no-one is open to discussion here.

Classes at the Try-out studio stimulate me and compensate for my frustrations. Teachers there are more on my wave length. I am also busily making sculptures for which I am receiving many commissions.

April 14th 1983

A five day tour of Germany is over. The theatre in Leverkusen was a large modern one and we had an orchestra playing for the performances which was a real treat as we usually dance to recorded music. One day we were free until the evening so I took a train to Düsseldorf to see the friends with whom I have kept in contact. It was lovely to see them, but as usual the town itself depressed me and I have never been so glad to return to Amsterdam.

I dream of gorgeous men and comforting cuddles regularly. This seems to help ease my loneliness in my romantic life.

April 18th 1983

My aunt from Den Haag invited me to see the famous display of tulips and other flowers at Keukenhof last weekend. It was most impressive; such a colourful array. I'm really glad to have had the chance to see this before leaving Holland.

I did a most enjoyable class at Try-out this evening. The pianist's inspired playing had a great influence. I complimented him afterwards and he was obviously flattered. He seems a really nice person and is English! He is one of the most interesting young men I have met in Amsterdam. He has a good sense of humour and sensitive musicality. He appears to have the qualities that I love in English people and miss here. Will I ever go home? Or even have a few more English friends around? I don't really harbour fantasies about him, well maybe just a little, but it gives me confidence to meet someone I take a real liking to. This is a yard stick for other encounters where I think there is something wrong with me if don't reciprocate a man's interest in me.

April 27th 1983

I received a nice letter today from the Swedish friends of my American cousin, Steve. They say they can't help me with accommodation and I'd do best to look for something when I am there. However, they offer me their spare room whilst I search, which I appreciate very much. The Opera House promised to find me a flat, but there has been no positive news yet.

May 4th 1983

Perhaps I have found something progressive in my final season with Scapino after all as I have decided to choreograph a piece for this year's choreographic workshop. People admire the sense of movement in my sculptures and a dancer friend suggested that I should do some choreo

raphy. I didn't believe I was capable of stringing two steps together, but after some consideration I have found a piece of music which arouses so much passion in my soul, and images of dance in my mind's eye, that it seems possible. The music is Gabriel Fauré's *Élégie* for piano and cello with Thomas Igloi as the cellist. The memory of Tom and his music gives me the strength to believe that I must at least give myself the chance to try and choreograph. Fauré's music gives me the structure and emotion. It will be a pas de deux, basically abstract, but saying something about the plight of the human spirit: loneliness, searching, finding and losing. Creative restlessness is eating me up inside. I must free it and here is my opportunity.

Casting is a tricky task, but I have chosen two young dancers who need to work to develop themselves. Cas and Julie are both tall and long limbed enabling them, hopefully, to adapt to my movements easily. They look good together which is also important They are both leaving the company at the end of the season and I can nurture their ambitions by challenging them in *Élégie*.

May 9th 1983

I'm totally consumed and obsessed by my choreography. It's so exciting to try something new and discover so much movement flowing from my body. Cas and Julie like the music and show enthusiasm for my movements and ideas. It's going to be rewarding working with them and we are all going to learn a lot. I can see the potential in their bodies to do what I want and I shall enjoy the challenge of drawing it out of them.

May 12th 1983

I'm spending some time lying on my stomach with an ice pack on my bottom. This morning I was trying out some steps thinking "I wonder if Cas can do this?" in the middle of a pirouette, when I found myself on the floor. I've bruised myself just as I did when I fainted at Schipol airport. However, the choreography is tremendously fulfilling. Everyday I find new movements, shapes and ideas; it's so thrilling. I've made designs for the costumes and see them in subtle earthy colours: shades of brown, orange, green ... I'm more inspired in my own dancing again and love it when the English pianist plays for classes at Try-out and my limbs are in harmony with the music.

May 17th 1983

It is like Christmas! Armando has agreed to let me go home for a week when I have no performances or rehearsals so that I can maintain contact with Festival Ballet in the hope that I might be able to go there from Sweden. What a wonderful excuse to go home!

The process of creation is both exciting and exhausting. It's fascinating to observe myself in this new role. I'm learning so much by throwing myself into this challenge. I discuss my ideas constantly with the dancers who accept my corrections on technical problems. They are sufficiently inexperienced to need help, yet experienced enough to know how to use it. It's interesting to watch my ballet developing and ideas drop from heaven at the least likely moments. I am progressing so quickly with *Élégie* that I am already thinking about doing a second piece for the workshop. I want to experiment with the plasticity of my own body; focusing on what it can do for a change, instead of stressing about what it can't do. I'm fed up of waiting for a choreographer to "discover" me and show the world my qualities. I am constantly astonished by the resources of ideas and vocabulary of movement I possess. People are surprised when I tell them the new solo will be barefoot and to the sound of birdsong. I have always loved the sound of birds singing and chirping. This is my inspiration and starting point for the new piece. I also want to incorporate some poses from oriental dancing which I have long admired.

June 3rd 1983

I've calmed down considerably after a week at home during which I had the dreaded cold. I was not allowed to take class with Festival Ballet, but I tried to corner John Field backstage one day to maintain personal contact. There was panic and confusion in the corridors by the stage door, because a cast list for that evening's performance named the men instead of the women in the company to dance the swans in Acts Two and Four of *Swan Lake*! No-one was interested in me with such pandemonium.

June 10th 1983

Élégie is almost finished. It's amazing to watch my ideas come to life before my eyes and also to observe the dancers grow and develop through the creative process. I constantly surprise myself by my ability to invent movements which look pleasing, and am a little overwhelmed by the way the piece is taking on an identity over which I no longer have complete control. Everyone is most supportive, from the dancers to the lighting technician and wardrobe mistress. I still get very excited about it and have difficulty controlling my emotions. It is like being in love. Consequently I sometimes feel absolutely washed out. I've decided not to show *Birdsong*. It is far from finished and I need time to explore my ideas. So I'll concentrate on *Élégie* for now which still needs a lot of work before it's polished enough for presentation.

A letter arrived today from the Opera House in Stockholm confirming the date of the start of season and welcoming me. It was really comforting to receive this. I also got my Swedish working and residence permits stamped into my passport today. This period of working my notice, waiting to leave Amsterdam and start my new life in Stockholm, is very tedious. I'm itching to get on with my new life. But gradually Sweden is becoming more tangible.

June 19th 1983

I gave a big party yesterday to celebrate my quarter century as well as my new contract. I was surprised how well my room and balcony absorbed everyone. The monthly blues drained my energy and I felt spaced out most of the time. Luckily everyone seemed to enjoy themselves.

June 21st 1983

The sun came out and my birthday has been a very hot day. I think this is one of my nicest birthdays ever, and a special present was a letter from Stockholm informing me that a flat has been found for me. It's furnished, a reasonable price, and belongs to a clarinettist in the orchestra.

Although *Élégie* is coming along well, I realise that it lacks artistic flair and needs light and shade in the interpretation. So today I decided to push my dancers and try to achieve this. They do not give it to me naturally, I have to coax it from them. By the final run through I could see sparks of what I want, but Julie has difficulty feeling what she is doing and therefore does not know when she is doing what I want. She was in tears at the end. God! Why do there always have to be tears? Anyway I think the result was positive and we were able to discuss the problems.

My Swedish continues to progress. I have completed another grammar book and read magazines lent to me by a Swedish girl in the company. She is unwilling to speak Swedish with me because she is from the south and speaks with a different dialect from that spoken in Stockholm.

July 3rd 1983

My last performance with Scapino was surprisingly emotional. There were the traditional jokes and it was hard to maintain concentration whilst splitting one's sides laughing at someone else's stupidities. A green head-dress had been made for me to replace my usual white one in *Humoresque* and the dancers insisted I wear it. One boy wore dark glasses through the entire piece. My contribution was change to "Take 1" and "Take 2", in my part with the movie camera, to "Take 183" and "Take 184". This was the correct number of performance "Takes" (92 performances since the premiere). Then I played the section in the spirit of a tired, bored prima donna after almost two hundred takes. Usually I am lifted high by my partner at the end, but this time it had been arranged, unknown to me of course, for a lighting technician to come onstage pick me up and carry me off! Many unscheduled things happened and I found it quite nerve wracking because I never knew what would happen next. The audience of children loved it all, oblivious of the changes in the choreography. I don't think the ballet master with us dared to say anything.

July 11th 1983

I have been feeling very deflated since my last performance in Holland. The battle to lose weight continues. It seems considerably more difficult since my periods returned. I feel I am fighting against nature all the time. I am just under 51 kilos now but really need to get down to 49. Coping with the hunger seems especially hard right now.

Watching a performance of *Giselle* by Dutch National Ballet reminded me that I am going to a large classical company. It will be so different from Scapino.

July 14th 1983

I was thrilled at the dress rehearsal this evening. It was pure magic when the curtain opened on *Élégie*. The mauve horizon was atmospheric and Cas looked like a Greek God before it. The costumes looked lovely and the dancers performed artistically and smoothly. I swallowed back tears all the way through and by the end they were rolling down my cheeks. I hugged Julie and Cas together afterwards and thanked them.

I've already received many compliments on *Élégie* and my production of the dancers. Apparently I brought out hidden qualities in them. I shall leave Amsterdam victorious, eager to commence my contract with the Royal Swedish Ballet after a short holiday at home.

Chapter Five

Stockholm   Part One

1983 - 1984

August 9th 1983

So here I am in Sweden. Of course the reality of it all is quite unlike my fantasy, but the effort I made to prepare myself was well worthwhile. I would feel very lost if I couldn't understand any Swedish, even though the Swedes speak excellent English.

I sailed to Gothenburg from England on a rather luxurious boat with sauna, swimming pool and cinema. Then I took a train to Stockholm where Mia (the friend of Steve, my American cousin) met me and drove me some kilometres outside of Stockholm to where she lives with her husband and their two small daughters.

Mia's family, and her parents who live in central Stockholm, have received me with great warmth. They obviously have the highest regard for Steve and because of this are especially hospitable to me. I really appreciate how welcome they have made me. The big surprise was to meet Steve at Mia's parents' flat as he had flown to Stockholm this weekend. It seemed surreal to see him here, and his familiar face helped me feel more at ease.

I spent the weekend with Mia and her family enjoying the idyllic countryside where they live. Mia drove me into town on Monday morning to do class at the Opera House and collect the key to my flat. There is a week of voluntary classes before rehearsals commence which gives me a chance to settle in. The weather is fantastic and I feel on holiday as I explore the Swedish capital.

I went on a boat trip today around the city's islands. The views from the water are magnificent. There is so much to do here during the summer months of June, July and August. I am told it is much quieter the rest of the year. The modern centre of the city is full of shopping complexes. Everything looks so attractive, inviting one to buy. The island of the Old Town (Gamla Stan) is where Stockholm originated. The iron mining industry gradually drew people out to live on the neighbouring islands. Now these islands are residential areas of colourful houses. My flat is on the South Island (Södermalm), conveniently situated ten minutes by underground from the centre of town and the Opera House.

My flat is small, but will be cosy when I've been able to make it feel like home. There is a small hallway, a bathroom (with a bath tub thank goodness), a small kitchen with a table and chairs (so for the first time I will be able to use my kitchen as a second living space and dining room), and a bed sitting room with two single beds. The flat is fully furnished, adequately for my needs. There is a large black and white television set and a telephone. Once my belongings arrive I think I shall feel quite at home here. My local supermarket is open every day, including Sundays, from 9am to 9pm. It sells many Swedish products, as well as Danish and Finnish imports. There is so much for me to try. I have to go shopping with my dictionary or I might try cooking with washing powder instead of salt! I bought some plants which add atmosphere to the flat.

The Swedish people seem strange to me, like fantasy characters: gnomes and vikings. Many are fair and they have a distinctive look. They exude a sense of contentment, which is understandable considering the high standard of living they enjoy here.

I have found a place for myself in the dressing rooms at the theatre. Backstage is unbelievably luxurious, and apparently it has only recently been renovated. Even with such a large company, there are only six places in each dressing room, and corps de ballet share with soloists. Each room has a lounge area with a coffee table, sofa and kettle, and every floor has its own refrigerator. There is an abundance of showers. People seem friendly and relaxed; no wonder with such comforts available.

August 11th 1983

When I wake up in the mornings I am disorientated and a strange feeling comes over me when I remember where I am. I'm still overwhelmed every time I go into town by the splendour of it all, and it gives me an enormous thrill to go to work at such a regal Opera House.

The air is wonderfully fresh here. Sometimes I wake up in the night, lean out of the window, and take a deep breath. It feels so healthy.

Today I visited Skansen. This is a huge open air museum of Swedish architecture. It is an ideal place to visit in the summer with its spacious grounds and different kinds of houses. There are also various entertainments and I watched some folk dancing. The Swedes make the most of their rich folk traditions.

August 13th 1983

It's pouring with rain; a sudden change in the weather. Everyone says summer is over now. I certainly hope they are wrong. Anyway I have the satisfaction of knowing that I made the most of the sunshine last week.

I'm beginning to notice the less positive aspects of life in Sweden. The Swedes are not a lively and cheerful nation. I find some of their "artistic" underground station decors very dark and oppressive. I'm also aware of a lot of alcoholics roaming the streets. The Scandinavian drinking problem is no myth. I suspect the Swedes of being narrow minded. Not only do Stockholmers look down on people from other parts of Sweden, but the people in the south of town would not dream of moving to the north, and vice versa. Perhaps this is an attitude of people isolated on the islands, as they were before the bridges were built. Even now, many of the islands of the archipelago are only accessible by water.

It's like a jungle in my flat now that my twenty-eight boxes from Amsterdam have been delivered. But it will be like Christmas when I unpack them all!

August 14th 1983

Yesterday I was taken out by an acquaintance of a Dutch cousin. I have been so lucky to have introductions to Swedish people. It would certainly be very difficult to meet them otherwise. This young man, and a friend of his, took me to a popular meeting place in the city centre. It is a weird setting and was once a variety theatre. I felt removed, as if watching a film. I couldn't relate to the bizarre atmosphere of this place. I was surrounded by gnomes and Vikings.

It was interesting to speak with this Swede, who speaks perfect English. He assured me that I need not feel threatened by the drunks. They are unhappy people, but not usually violent. It would be against their proud nature to be aggressive towards a foreigner, especially an English one.

The Swedish people appear rather odd to me, but I suppose I shall grow accustomed to them. I seem to be liked and accepted as a foreigner, but can't imagine that I shall ever feel I belong here. It is strange to me that these Scandinavian people are geographically so close, yet mentally so different from other Europeans.

The underground trains run until two in the morning, when they are quite full. This place overflows with the unexpected.

This evening I went to Mia for dinner and met Steve there; another flight to Stockholm. He is starting to be more like a Swedish cousin than an American one. I really appreciated the family atmosphere in contrast to the Stockholm youth of yesterday. I am privileged to sample both.

August 17th 1983

As all beginnings, I felt uncomfortable in my first rehearsals today. The dancers are really just remembering the choreography after the holidays, making it difficult to learn by watching and copying. At one point I was supposed to be in three studios at once for rehearsals of *Rapport* and *Miss Julie* by the Swedish choreographer Birgit Culberg, and an opera *Sidharta*. I have been told to learn *Rapport* first. I'm just a cover for corps de ballet parts. All I can hope to do is familiarise myself with the music and shape of the choreography. I am trying to learn from videos as well. It's rather disorientating not to be able to get my teeth into anything, but patience is an essential ingredient to survive the first weeks of any new job. No-one appears to be in the routine of working yet. I suppose that is understandable after two months' vacation.

Rehearsals are from 11.30am (after one and a half hours class) till 3.30pm with forty-five minutes for lunch plus short breaks. When there is a performance they finish at 1pm, as in Germany. Sometimes, before a premiere, there are evening calls from 7pm to 10pm. Anything else counts as paid overtime.

There are quite a lot of older dancers as it's normal to dance here till the age of forty-five and then retire and receive a pension. Young dancers only have a hope of promotion if a senior soloist or principal retires. Many corps de ballet members dance solo and leading roles and receive extra remuneration for this. It's not easy to meet your colleagues with everyone separated into all those dressing rooms, and people are involved in different rehearsals at different times in different places.

I took a bus to Sigtuna, one of the oldest towns in Sweden, and this made a refreshing break.

August 18th 1983

I'm doing my best to learn the repertoire from rehearsals and videos, and Gunilla Roempke (the director) clarified the situation for me today. She hopes I understand that it's normal to be a cover when starting with this company, everyone has their places in the ballets. However, I will be cast in the new production of *Nutcracker* in November. She made a point of telling me how happy she is that I am in the company. She treats me respectfully as though I am special. I do think I have special qualities, but can't fathom how she can know that without putting me through the customary tests and hoops. She also told me that I help to bridge the gap between the young inexperienced dancers and the older ones. There are few dancers in the mid-twenties age group in the company. This is the time when they are most likely to take the three-year leave of absence to which they are entitled, in order to broaden their experience elsewhere.

Somehow, quite unintentionally, I found myself mentioning my interest in participating in an International Competition. Dancers from the Royal Swedish Ballet have taken part in competitions before and it should be possible for me to do so if I wish. First, I must decide which competition to enter. There is a new one in Helsinki next year which sounds promising. Also, I must choose the repertoire to prepare, and if I want to present myself with a partner, I shall have to find one. This is tricky because I don't know the company yet. It's still early to make decisions; I was just sowing the seeds of an idea.

August 19th 1983
More time spent in the video room and I am feeling more confident about knowing the ballets. I watched the whole of *Rapport* and was most impressed by it. The use of lights and bodies communicates a theme of conflict between poverty and wealth. In the end everyone disappears through a tunnel of light, which I interpret to mean that rich and poor alike will die eventually. I have seen *Miss Julie* before and I have enormous respect for Birgit Culberg's work based on the Strindberg play. There will be a big celebration for her 75th birthday next month.

I've also watched the video of Jiri Kylian's *Ariadne*. It is a stunning piece for seven women; dramatic, with wonderfully sculptural, organic movements. I dream of dancing in that ballet. Unfortunately, it's not scheduled to be performed this season, so there is no hope for me.

I feel I'm going to involve myself in a lot of work this year. I have the appetite of a starved person, and I'm cultivating discipline. The latter is one of the few things which comes tax free here! I love the Opera House and like to be alone in the studios, video room or dressing room when everyone else has gone after 3.30pm. It all belongs to me then.

Nonetheless, when I go home alone, I'm prone to introspection. Sometimes I find tranquility within, but it is so transient. It settles for a brief moment and as I catch up with it, it flits away somewhere else.

August 21st 1983
It was a beautiful Sunday so I decided to go to the permanent exhibition of sculptures by Carl Milles on the island of Lidingö; Millesgården. It is imposing and inspiring with the massive sculptures in an outdoor setting. I passed through a moment of loneliness when I wished I could

103

share the experience with someone, but the mood passed and in the afternoon I took a boat to Drottningholm Palace. This is magnificent with perfectly proportioned buildings and lavish gardens. Traditionally it's the summer residence of the Royal family, the winter one being the palace on the central island of the Old Town in Stockholm.

August 24th 1983

New employees of the Opera House (650 people work here) were given a tour of the theatre. I was disappointed that there was no real opportunity to talk to each other as I listened to long speeches in Swedish. However, it was nice to be shown around and share their pride in the new hydraulic powered machinery for moving sets and computerised lighting system.

I've met my landlord and his family who live quite close to my flat in a larger apartment. They are friendly and I'm relieved to know that I can keep the flat for a year. Most Stockholmers seem to live in apartments in large buildings, old and new. One has to move out of town in order to have an entire house.

September 4th 1983

My first performance with the Royal Swedish Ballet fell from heaven much sooner than anticipated, as I danced a wealthy lady in *Rapport*. There was a magical atmosphere, not only for me but for everyone, as we celebrated Birgit Culberg's 75th birthday. She was brought onstage and applauded at the end in recognition of her long, renowned career. It was a full house with a very warm public. Performing on the beautiful stage of the Opera House was thrilling and my body so felt so much better performing in the evening instead of during the day as was often the case in Holland.

This evening brought another cosy dinner with Mia and her family, her parents and Steve who was here yet again. Steve's warmth and affection for me help to compensate for the emptiness I feel of missing home and my parents.

September 9th 1983

I shall be onstage again sooner than expected as I now have to dance in the Polonaise in the last act of John Cranko's *Onegin*. It's my luck that a tall girl has fallen sick and it has been noticed that I learn quickly.

Generally, rehearsals here are efficient with an emphasis on style and artistry. This is a welcome contrast from Scapino Ballet where there was more concentration on technique and everyone looking the same. A mixture of English and Swedish is spoken.

John Neumeier is here to cast a triple bill of his ballets to be shown later in the season. It must be tricky for him with so many faces to choose from. I wonder what he will be like to work with. He has such charisma.

September 11th 1983

My eczema has suddenly broken out badly, reflecting the turmoil of emotions I undergo in reaction to my new surroundings. I am slower to accept the changes than I thought I would be. I'm very disorientated and my concentration sometimes falters. I must pull myself together and establish a sense of order in my life. Conflicts arise in my aspirations amongst other things. I still long to dance in England, but do not savour the idea of the gruelling work schedule and touring which are typical of English companies. I am tempted by the security and comfort here; why should I drive myself to join a vicious rat race? But can I allow myself to stay here, collect cobwebs and become a little complacent like everyone else? All this speculation, and I have no idea if I'll be offered another contract anyway.

September 14th 1983

Another performance of *Onegin* brought another magical evening. It's such a rich production with superb music by Tchaikovsky and powerful drama. The audience was responsive, and there was applause as the curtain rose on the dancers in the third act poised in front of the elaborate background of a ballroom, as we waited to commence the Polonaise. It really is exciting and an honour to be a part of it all. I may be tempted to feel demoted by dancing in the corps de ballet, but I enjoy dancing without getting nervous about technically demanding roles. Gunilla was obviously pleased with the performance and thanked me personally for my contribution, which amazed me.

I've started Swedish lessons which are offered free of charge to all foreigners. Sometimes I cannot attend if they overlap with rehearsals. We are all different nationalities from: Brazil, Austria, Spain, France, Holland and England. The Dutch girl was delighted when I spoke Dutch with her.

September 15th 1983

I received another compliment on my dancing today, this time from the choreologist who rehearses many of the ballets as well as notating them. She told me how nice it is to see someone in the corps de ballet with the correct feeling for style and historical period. I was most flattered.

A dancer in the company is trying to organise a choreographic workshop for those who want to have the chance to choreograph. This is a novel idea here, but well timed for me as I need some extra work.

So I am working on my solo *Birdsong*, but find it hard to choreograph pure movement for its own sake with no motivation from music or drama. The curtain will open to the sound of birds singing and the dancer, centre stage, will be performing a small repetitive movement representative of walking. When the mood has been set, the dancer will suddenly fall into a series of contrasting dynamics which I intend to be controlled and elastic. Each movement should grow out of the one preceding it and flow into the next. The lack of a predetermined form or shape presents problems for me to solve as I go along. It's also challenging as I choreograph on my own body and can't see what I am doing. I know I want my audience to be captured by the variety and unexpectedness of the movements. I suppose it's a kind of intellectual exploration of the possibilities of the human body in a rather sculptural way. I'm not sure if I should do it myself or ask another dancer to do it, and if so who? I'm apprehensive about asking someone else partly because I don't know the personalities or dancing of my colleagues well yet, and partly because I'm not certain about my own creative ideas. I'd like to challenge my own body, but I'm also nervous at the idea of performing my own choreography. I was a nervous wreck watching it, what would I be like performing it? Also, it's lonelier to do it alone and there is a definite drawback in not being able to see the choreography.

September 16th 1983

I received praise again from my director after another performance of *Onegin*. She told me I am "beautiful; lovely to watch". It really is rather overwhelming, even though I am totally aware of what I am projecting onstage. A mixture of inspiration and experience enables me to achieve this. I enjoy fantasies whilst dancing, imagining the atmosphere of nineteenth century Russian aristocracy and I think about cream: rich, thick, gooey cream like the white gloves we wear and the quality of movement in the dances. My partner looks noble with his moustache and I like to flirt with him during the performance.

It seems that one is judged by one's performance onstage in this company, not by one's achievements in class or rehearsals. This is logical to me, but it's not always the case. Every company functions so differently. Perhaps in Scapino it was the direction's insecurity which caused them to lay so much importance on meticulous work in the ballet studio. Certainly, results onstage were well drilled, but sometimes lacking in spontaneity. Things are different here where the Royal Swedish Ballet has a historical tradition dating back over 200 years, and employees of the Opera House have the comfort of security. There is some complacency it's true but, where performances are concerned, the dancers have their sense of responsibility to their profession.

September 21st 1983

Peter Appel is here from Basle to mount Heinz Spoerli's production of *Nutcracker* and he is also giving us wonderful classes. I like his philosophy, "dancing is about life, and life is about progress." In the slow controlled movements of adage he tell us to save our energy, "don't get sentimental girls!"

Heinz Spoerli is also here for a few days. It is strange to be working with him after auditioning for him twice. I am getting more variety here than I would in Basle where most of the repertoire is by Spoerli.

September 23rd 1983

An amended cast list for *Nutcracker* informs me that as well as being in Waltz of the Flowers, cover for Snowflakes and the ball in Act One, I am also third cast for the Arabian Dance in Act Two. The latter is for three tall women and one shorter man and gives me my first chance to step out of the corps de ballet. I am delighted about this.

I met my neighbour today as a letter from England addressed to her was mistakenly delivered through my door. I decided to ring her doorbell and give her the letter. She is a middle-aged English woman who married a Swede. At last I have met someone from my block of flats, and what a coincidence that she should be English. When I invited her to tea later she told me her life story and I realised that she is possibly lonelier than I am. She suffered a stroke a few years ago and as a result is partially paralysed. She is divorced and has a son my age who is a medical student in Northern Sweden. I am so glad to have met her. I feel less isolated now I know who my neighbour if. I miss not having close friends or family so much. I miss cuddles too.

September 30th 1983

I started learning the Arabian Dance today. It's good to have something extra to work on and I like the sensual movements. I don't know if or when I'll get a performance. I guess a lot depends on how soon someone gets sick or injured. I'll be waiting …

October 9th 1983

The King and Queen of Sweden came to the performance this evening and the orchestra played the national anthem. It was special for me but everyone else took it very much in their stride, including the extra bow to the Royal box.

Gradually I seem to making routines for myself, and work at finding distractions. I like to get on any bus and go to the end stop just for the sake of it. Visits to the cinema are also a favourite pastime. All films are in their original language here with Swedish subtitles. It's very important to me to hear English. My neighbour and Mia are becoming good friends.

October 12th 1983

I'm getting itchy feet already! I don't know what is the matter with me, but I feel restless again. Certainly it's healthy for me to keep "on my toes" and I think that the secret to happy survival for me here will be to mentally keep one foot constantly out of the door, my suitcase half packed. If I submit to the security and satisfaction of the Swedish social security system which is very evident within the company, I'll be lost.

October 17th 1983

Something extraordinary has happened. Heinz Spoerli is back again and I have been told he wants to take me out of Waltz of the Flowers. The ballet staff are confused, and want to keep me in. I am staggered by the whole affair.

Autumn in Sweden is short, but colourful. The golds and reds seem very intense.

October 21st 1983

I'm still rehearsing Waltz of the Flowers in the midst of a battle between the choreographer and the management. What did I do to deserve this?

I've stared working with weights to tone up the muscles in my legs more. All the equipment is provided in a special gym room at the Opera House. It is worth taking advantage of. I have to remind myself that I am involved in an athletic activity requiring a preoccupation with one's physical condition.

October 28th 1983

I've started speaking onto cassette tapes and sending them to my parents as well as writing regularly. This is an alternative to speaking on the telephone which is very expensive; much more so than when I was in

Holland and Germany. It is wonderful to hear their voices when they send their recordings to me and I listen to them over and over again.

There was a dramatic rehearsal of Waltz of the Flowers today beginning with tears from a girl who was suddenly taken out by Spoerli. Then he called me up to him. I approached in trepidation. To my amazement he told me that he thinks I am very talented and have a nice figure, but I could push myself more. He also mentioned something about the English style being too reserved. The rehearsal continued with another girl being insulted about her weight resulting in more tears.

Spoerli's words gave me food for thought and it occurred to me that I might change my attitude to my work. In recent years I have worked hard because I thought I was not good enough and had negative attitudes about my abilities. My new, positive way of thinking, is to see work as a means of nurturing my talent.

Gunilla Roempke is leaving at the end of this season and the dancers are interviewing prospective candidates for her post. This is another new experience for me, where dancers have an influence over their management. I have sat in on all the interviews and find them fascinating, though I have been unable to contribute much as it's still all so new to me.

October 30th 1983

My neighbour introduced me to Skärholmen today. It is one of the famous modern suburbs of Stockholm with tower blocks of flats and spacious shopping precincts and is quite a tourist attraction. I found it barren and soulless and am thankful not to have to live there.

November 2nd 1983

The premiere of *Nutcracker* seemed to go well and Heinz Spoerli was especially pleased with Waltz of the Flowers! It is nerve wracking to do only this number in the performance as one has to wait so long till almost the end of the ballet, and then rush around the stage dancing some tricky combinations nonstop for seven minutes.

I notice I have picked up a company trait of drifting through classes and not being totally concentrated. I must be alert, and can start by learning the exercises properly in class which I have sometimes been slack about. I would cheat by watching someone who has learnt them out of the corner of my eye. Part of the problem is that I don't enjoy my free time enough. I tend to see free time as a threat, a big black hole which I don't know how to fill, and I feel very out of control. Rather than focussing more when I'm dancing, I get into a habit of drifting through everything. When my period is due I am more prone to depression, fatigue, lack of concentration and my diet becomes harder to control. But my periods are very irregular, so I never know what is going on. Although I'm never satisfied with my body, I'm not fat. My weight has been about 50 - 51 kilos recently, but I'm painfully aware that I was less when I auditioned.

To my surprise I have dreamed of my Dutch ex-boyfriend several times since arriving here. I would love to have a male companion, but when am I ever going to meet anyone? And yet I am also a little afraid of the complications of a relationship.

November 7th 1983

I did the Snowflakes, as well as Waltz of the Flowers this evening. This made the evening longer and more satisfying.

Another speciality of this country was revealed to me when I discovered that unemployed and freelance dancers are provided with classes free of charge by the government. I really think I'm on another planet sometimes!

November 13th 1983

A date has been set for the choreographic workshop performance in January. It will be in the Rotundan, a small open stage in the Opera House building, and will be presented to an invited audience. I have decided to present *Élégie* as well as *Birdsong*. I shall dance the latter myself, but there is the issue of casting the former. I shall choose young dancers again.

Extracts from *Nutcracker* were shown on television and it was strange to be able to pick myself out. However, I am beginning to get used to watching myself on the small screen as dress rehearsals and many performances are video recorded. This is a useful way of checking one's work.

It has turned very cold, below freezing, and Christmas decorations are out in the shopping streets.

November 16th 1983

The marathon of *Nutcracker* performances is over and I'm into a quieter period again. Most of the corps de ballet has an easy time as Valery Panov is choreographing *Three Sisters*, and it involves mostly soloists.

I have a lot of pain in my hips again and even massage is not helping. I expect it will pass eventually.

November 20th 1983

A chat with Gunilla about my future in the company did not satisfy me as I had hoped. Although she compliments me on the quality of my work and my professional approach, she will not know if contracts are available for next season for another month.

Work on *Élégie* and *Birdsong* is most rewarding. This gives me a sense of purpose which is hard to maintain when I dance in the corps de ballet. Luckily, I have recorded *Élégie* on video, making the job of reproducing it relatively easy. Choreography is so absorbing and no dance experience has ever given me so much pleasure as creating movement. It seems such a natural thing to me to do that I don't know why I didn't do it before. It's so much easier than dancing other people's steps; I feel like I am cheating. I never would have dreamed when I started on *Élégie* in Amsterdam that it was the beginning of a new and exciting process of discovery, or that it would be so important in helping me on my way spiritually and professionally in Stockholm.

December 7th 1983

I was sorry to hear of the death of Erich Walter. Apparently, he had been suffering from leukaemia for some time. Perhaps that is the reason his moods were so unpredictable when I worked in Düsseldorf.

I did the ball scene in Act One in *Nutcracker* this evening and it makes a tremendous difference to be so much more involved in the performance. This scene is great fun, wearing the gorgeous dresses with bare shoulders and ringlets hanging onto them. I love to be elegant.

I'm constantly toying with the possibilities of staying or leaving at the end of my contract. I waste a tremendous amount of mental energy debating the pros and cons with myself which, considering I don't even know if I'll be offered another contract, is quite silly.

The first snow has fallen and Stockholm looks picturesque. It is cold between -5 and -10°C but it's not damp, so I don't feel as cold as I thought I would.

We are rehearsing for the Neumeier programme and I'm cast in the group of *Tristan and Isolde* as one of twelve barefoot women representing the sea. I've also been chosen by Neumeier's assistant, Ilse Wiedman, who is teaching us the ballets, to learn a part in *Die Stille* to weird music by George Crumb. This is a modern style, on pointe, for a small cast of soloists.

December 13th 1983

At last I am busy and it is satisfying. Many people are sitting around with little to occupy them. I am doing all three corps de ballet parts in *Nutcracker*, sometimes in different places, and rehearsing the Neumeier programme, as well as fitting my choreography in between. Everyone involved in the workshop has to grab the studios whenever they are free. The quietest time is after 1pm on performance days.

Today the Swedes celebrate Santa Lucia in traditional fashion. Processions commence early in the morning with young girls dressed in white, some wearing crowns of burning candles. There is a lot of singing of traditional songs and drinking of glögg (mulled wine). These festivities help to brighten up the long dark winter days.

December 27th 1983

It was absolutely wonderful to be able to spend five days at home over Christmas. I am very seriously considering returning to England next season, even if it leaves me financially insecure. I took a class with Festival Ballet and felt that my way of dancing belongs at home and will only blossom there. I also need emotional security in order for my talent to grow. Being homesick and lonely is not fruitful for my soul. I fear the emptiness of being alone more than unemployment.

The Plant

There is a patch of earth
In this soil seeds were sown
A plant began to grow
The plant battled with the seasons of life
It survived until one day
It was plucked from the ground
And placed in some foreign soil
The plant began to wilt
Beaten by unknown weathers
It was blown to other places
Until it discovered how to lay roots
Then it had a chance to breathe
New buds sprang forth
But before these buds can truly blossom
The plant must be returned to its own soil.

December 30th 1983

I have been offered another year's contract in a meeting with the direction. The future is unclear as most of next year's planning depends on Egon Madsen, the new director. Gunilla obviously likes me, but I shall have to re-establish myself with a new director.

We also discussed solos I could take to the competition in Helsinki. Just choosing what to do involves a lot of homework before rehearsals even commence. I will need four classical variations and two contemporary ones. Gunilla told me that she is impressed by my beautiful arms, quality, sense of dance and intelligent way of working. The only criticism is of my famous bottom. She suggested I could fine down a little and strengthen my technique by pulling up more through the buttock muscles. Even though I agree with her, I feel deflated to hear her words. I feel embarrassed and ashamed that for all my intelligence and dedication I still have the same faults. I know nothing can be hidden in class. She really was very nice about it and assured me that even the principals need "reminders" occasionally. I know she only wants to help, and I appreciate her time and concern. I just wish I could be perfect and not need "reminders".

January 17th 1984

I saw New Year 1984 in with dancers from the company. At midnight we went out to the waterfront of the old town and let off fireworks. As in Holland, New Year's Eve is firework night in Sweden.

I've been promoted to first cast of the Arabian Dance in *Nutcracker* replacing a dancer who has leave of absence. Work is very busy and I'm definitely second cast in *Die Stille*. Gunilla's chat with me gave me the push I needed to shed a kilo and I am now back to 49 kilos and my periods have stopped.

My social life is a little fuller as I start to feel more comfortable with my colleagues, and I have a new friend outside of the theatre. I met Alex on the plane returning from London. He is from New Zealand, the same age as me, and had spent Christmas with his sister in London. He has just started work in Stockholm as a computer programmer at the racetrack at Solvalla. Luckily for him, friends of his from New Zealand have come over at the same time. Alex is a good companion for me. We seem to have enough shared interests to enjoy each other's company, and sufficient differences to extend our experiences.

My parents are planning visits to Stockholm this year giving me something to look forward to.

January 21st 1984

Today must have been one of my most nerve wracking and terrifying experiences ever with a matinee of *Nutcracker*, and the workshop. I was less nervous for the dress rehearsal of the workshop yesterday, even though John Neumeier watched then. This evening Richard Collins (ballet master from Festival Ballet who is currently guest teacher), Valery Panov and Birgit Culberg were in the audience, not to mention all the people from the Opera House. I just wanted to run away. I'm so relieved it's all over now.

I have received a staggering amount of positive feedback on my choreography; mostly on *Birdsong*. I remember the way I started on this solo and the exercises I put myself through to get it together; the pain of trying out unfamiliar movements, and the frustrations and doubts. Sometimes I wondered if I would dare to do it at all. But I did dare, and I never could have dreamed or hoped for such an overwhelmingly enthusiastic response. Gunilla suggested I take *Birdsong* to the competition in Helsinki as a contemporary solo.

January 25th 1984

New cast lists for the Neumeier programme have gone up and in addition to the parts I was already cast for, I am now third cast for the principal role of Brangäne in *Tristan and Isolde*. I feel very honoured, though this promotion does not help my social life in the company. Envy is subdued here, but I am still a relative outsider and it is disconcerting for established members of the company to see me given so many opportunities so soon.

Steve visited again. As usual it was lovely to see him and I can confide in him too which is very helpful. He warned me that my longing to return home might blind me to the realities and I might be disappointed.

My parents have persuaded me to accept a second year's contract despite my doubts, in the hope that this will encourage the direction to help me to prepare myself for Helsinki. I can hardly expect an interest to be taken in me if I show that I plan on leaving. I do want to do the competition very much. It will take place during the summer holidays. Although next year's repertoire remains undecided, the tour to Lapland scheduled in the autumn appeals to me.

I have been out with Alex several times but there seems to be a conflict in our desires. He wants romance, I want a friend. I am simply too involved in my work right now for emotional ties. I feel I must put everything into my work if I hope to achieve any success. Distraction is dangerous. It's difficult for him to understand this. I also feel I need to get to know him better before embarking on a physical relationship. He strikes me as immature and somehow I don't feel really attracted to him with his pale blue eyes and brown hair. I hope we can remain friends as his companionship is important to me.

It is still very cold, but the snow is pretty.

February 1st 1984

I feel encouraged to continue choreographing since my success in the workshop, and to play with all sorts of ideas in my mind. It might take some time for these to materialise as I'm so involved with rehearsals and preparing for Helsinki. After seeing the video of *Birdsong*, I realise I can perform the movements much more slowly and savour them more. I seemed to rush through it in order to get it over with as quickly as possible.

February 6th 1984

My new contract arrived by post today. I'm still unsure about the decision to sign it.

An exhibition of paintings of exotic birds at the modern art museum reminded me of *Birdsong*. The steps seem to suggest birds to me, and to others also, yet I never intended this. It is strange how the choreography has taken on a life of its own.

February 15th 1984

Not only is it wonderful to have my father's company, but he has given my flat a facelift by rearranging the furniture. It feels like new. It's good he can occupy himself as we are very busy with evening rehearsals as well as the usual ones till 3.30pm.

John Neumeier is here now until the premiere. He has a rare magnetism and is the only person I have witnessed hold the attention of every member of the Royal Swedish Ballet. You could hear a pin drop when he is speaking. The dancers are never so respectful of anyone else. He is incredibly inspiring to work with.

We have also started rehearsing *Giselle*. I am cast in the corps de ballet in both acts. I had hoped for more, but of course others must be given opportunities as well.

Steve was in Stockholm and met my father for the first time. Strange that they must travel to Sweden from London and Seattle in order to meet!

February 20th 1984

This morning I managed to pluck up the courage to speak to John Neumeier. I told him how inspiring it has been to work with him. I was apprehensive about approaching him, but the strength of the feeling that I must talk to him outweighed my fears. There was an immediate rapport and he took the opportunity to tell me how much he had liked my *Birdsong* solo. Apparently he had chosen me to learn the role of Brangäne after seeing it and he encouraged me to continue choreographing. He also said that he hopes I get a chance to perform Brangäne. I responded by telling him how very much I should like to do it, and suggested he drops a hint to the direction for me. He smiled knowingly and said he would do so. Then he wished me good luck and asked me if I am American!

February 28th 1984

The full rehearsal of *Giselle* with Galina Ulanova, who has been coaching the principals, should have been an auspicious occasion. She is one of the world's truly great ballerinas from the Bolshoi Ballet in Moscow, and is enormously respected as an artist. It is a great honour to have her as a guest ballet mistress. I had been very much looking forward to the session. Unfortunately, it was ruined by the general lack of concentration and commitment of the corps de ballet. Consequently, her words of wisdom were directed only to the soloists and I felt ashamed for the company that they did not appreciate her presence.

I've been told to learn the role of Emilia in José Limón's *The Moor's Pavane*. This is a brilliant piece of subtle dance drama for a quartet of dancers to music by Purcell. I love Limón's flowing, organic movements and am delighted to be able to work on it. I shall probably not have a chance to perform it as it is only being shown twice. It is quite awesome to be called for rehearsals with the company principals for both this, and Brangäne in *Tristan and Isolde*.

My energy is drained by a streaming cold. People keep asking if I'm crying. But I shall not give in; I don't want to miss anything.

March 8th 1984

The evenings are suddenly getting much longer and it does not get dark until about 6pm. There is a promise of spring after the long winter. You have to experience a Scandinavian winter to understand it. Words cannot adequately express the sensation of several months with only a few hours of daylight and up to six months of snow enveloping the ground with not a green shoot or bud in sight. And Stockholm is relatively south. In Lapland, above the Arctic Circle, there is no daylight at all

116

during the winter months. Of course this loss of sunshine is compensated for in the summer when it doesn't get dark at all. It must be strange to have no rhythm to the days which run into each other without punctuation when it is always dark, or always light.

I have started rehearsing properly for Helsinki and Richard Collins is coaching me. He is here as a guest teacher again. I like his classes very much. These, and his coaching are very helpful to me.

There are problems getting the costumes I need from the wardrobe department and recording the music. All these hassles are actually harder work than the dancing, but I'm determined to try and go to Helsinki. Gunilla is reasonably supportive but, having sat on juries, she is clearly not a believer in competitions. I know Art cannot be competitive, but I do not want to go there to win. I need the work that the preparation gives me, I want the stimulation of participating, and I need a goal to work for. Besides, it's a good excuse to visit Finland!

I am working very hard, often rehearsing through the day and performing at night. We have started *Giselle* performances now. Sometimes I start at 10am and finish at 11pm. But I'm so happy in my work, even though my feet get very sore from all the dancing on pointe. I get blisters on my toes and inflamed big toe joints. If my blisters bleed through the plasters I have put on them, sometimes they stick to my tights. The most efficient way to remove my tights then is to soak my feet, in the tights, in hot water until I can remove them easily. I have lost a kilo in weight through all the activity.

I was so hoping I might get a chance to dance the part of Brangäne. It is an interesting role and I have been working hard on it. I asked Gunilla if there might be an opening for me and she replied that there are so few performances that only the first and second casts will do it. When I asked not to be forgotten, I was assured that I would not be as my name is on the cast list. This isn't much appreciation for my attendance at rehearsals and extra work in my free time to prepare myself for all the parts I am cast for. At least I had the courage to ask.

March 15th 1984

These are happy days filled with work and a sense of purpose. We are learning *Swan Lake* and I enjoy being a swan in Acts Two and Four as the tall girls are at the front for a change. This is to give a greater sense of depth to the stage. I also do the Princess in a vision scene in Act One who is turned into a swan, and am second cast for the solo couple in the Mazurka in Act Three. *Swan Lake* promises to be happily busy without being nerve wracking.

117

I'm beginning to feel more optimistic about the possibility of staying next season. Surely I can gain and learn from Egon Madsen and the new influences he will bring?

My confidence is running high especially since Gunilla told me that John Neumeier has invited me to show *Birdsong* in Hamburg where he is the ballet director. A couple of other pieces from the workshop will also be shown. Nothing is definite yet, but just to be invited is a tremendous thrill. I don't think my apparent success in my work recently is helping me to make friends in the company. I probably seem very ambitious and single minded, and might appear a threat to some dancers. If only they knew I bury myself in work to escape the emptiness I otherwise feel.

Often I fantasise about the things I desire which might fill this void: to be home in England where I can understand the jokes on the radio, to have friends around me to spend my spare time with, and most of all to have a man to love, snuggle up to at night, cook dinners for and laugh together. But I have no way of controlling this aspect of my life, except to go home, where I am sure my social life would be easier to organise. So thoughts of home are continually in the back of my mind. And yet my work is intrinsic to my way of life, and here I have a wonderful working situation. I may have to forfeit that if I return to England. I may not even be able to get a job as a dancer. It is so much a matter of luck and timing. I'm torn in half between Stockholm and London.

March 23rd 1984

Last night I dreamed of a handsome stranger who seduced me. My bed was in a dreadful mess when I woke up and I floated through the day with a glowing feeling as if I were in love. Dreams such as this are a wonderful relief, letting me experience love and passion in my sleep. I almost felt as if the man I dreamed about had been sent by someone who is watching over me, God perhaps, to protect me from the destructiveness of my frustration.

My entry forms are on their way to Helsinki and my final decision on a programme of solos is: Round One - Giselle's Act One solo and Raymonda's Act Three solo; Round Two - *Birdsong*; Round Three - Odette's Act Two solo from *Swan Lake*, the Prelude from *Les Sylphides* and Olga's solo from Valery Panov's *Three Sisters*. I just hope my application is accepted.

April 1st 1984

Returning from a week's holiday at home I feel quite depressed to be back in Sweden. But I have a lot to look forward to, so hopefully my spirits will lift with the passing of time.

It was disappointing to receive a negative reply to my application for a grant to fund my trip to the competition in Helsinki. I shall have to pay for it myself. Luckily Helsinki is close to Stockholm. I suspect the reason I am not being helped is because I am not Swedish.

April 3rd 1984

Confirmation of the trip to Hamburg did much to revive my optimism.

I've learned Olga's solo in *Three Sisters* from the video and a choreologist will help me to rehearse it. The choreography is clear in my head, but I need help to teach it to my body which is slower to learn. It is such a beautiful solo, about Olga's yearning for more from life wishing she could fly away with the cranes. I relate to her emotions very easily.

We are performing every night at the moment, and when there is time I practise my variations for Helsinki.

April 7th 1984

Spring has arrived at last. It is like a miracle, one can almost watch the green buds bursting into leaf. It is +9°C and sunny. The nicest thing is to hear the running water of the streams which have been frozen all winter. Suddenly people are swarming the streets and one wonders if they have been in hibernation.

I'm starting to be very nervous about going to Hamburg and somewhat daunted by it all. The battle with my body continues. I'm not really fat at just under 49 kilos, but I look best as thin as possible.

John Renvall and Marianne Tcherkassy from American Ballet Theatre are guesting with us in *Giselle*. He is Swedish and went to America six years ago. They are both superb dancers and are an inspiration to watch. It is one of the huge advantages of this company to have so many world class guest dancers and teachers come to work with us.

April 12th 1984

Giselle is a little frustrating, especially the standing as a wili in Act Two. I hated it in Düsseldorf and I still hate it now. I'm not sure why standing decorating the stage in *Giselle* is so much worse than in any of the other "white" ballets, as those with sections of large corps de ballet in white costumes are known. However, in a few days time I shall fly to Hamburg and despite sore swollen toes, muscle cramps, sore eyes and a

119

general tiredness, I am optimistic. Many of the dancers are sick or injured, a typical phenomenon of the change of season from winter to spring which I have observed in every place I have danced.

I see Alex from time to time and one evening he brought a group of fifteen colleagues from his office to see a performance. I value his friendship very much.

April 19th 1984

I return triumphant and relieved from Hamburg. A group of six of us: dancers, choreographers and an administrator, flew out to Germany together. We stayed with various members of the direction of the Hamburg Ballet. I stayed with a ballet mistress. I found it somewhat overwhelming to be treated as a guest artist and to be invited to a small gathering at John Neumeier's home. It was also strange to dance *Birdsong* on the enormous stage of the Hamburg State Opera for an audience of almost two thousand. I felt rather lost but according to my colleagues, and the local newspapers, it went well. I was nervous but danced for John Neumeier and this gave me inspiration to carry me through.

Still unsure about my future in Stockholm, I pondered the possibility of auditioning for Hamburg Ballet sometime. Working for Neumeier would surely be a wonderful thing do and Hamburg as a city does have a certain charm and character. My feelings about returning to Germany are mixed, and starting somewhere new yet again wouldn't be easy. The most positive motivation is that it is half way back to London from Stockholm.

On my arrival back in Sweden I was greeted by my mother who has come to visit and awaited me in my flat. It felt like coming home.

My application to the Helsinki competition has been accepted, so I'm feeling happy about that. Now I'm thankful for a few days rest and the chance for my blisters, which have now become septic, to heal. I was warned by a doctor that I shouldn't dance on them in pointe shoes and I risked them developing gangrene.

April 28th 1984

My mother enjoyed her sight seeing in Stockholm and the performances she saw. I think she was particularly touched to see me dancing in such an impressive setting at the Opera House.

I'm now rehearsing my competition programme with Charles Mudry, the ballet master here.

May 3rd 1984

Sometimes life is like one big question mark. I have no sense of stability whatsoever. Perhaps it is because I'm an artist. The strong creative fire inside me seems to have surfaced more since I came to Sweden. People matter to me and it saddens me that I have difficulty in opening myself to them. I know I put barriers around myself. It tears at my gut that the people I love most are so far away. I long to fall in love, and yet I'm afraid of it too. I also fear that being alone too much will make it hard for me to relate to others. The world in my head closes up the more time I spend alone and the more my life revolves around myself. I am aware of the restrictions, yet unable to control them. I was once told that being alone is character building. Doubtless that is true to a certain extent, but an excess of solitude is soul destroying.

I am tired...

May 12th 1984

I'm enjoying performances of *Swan Lake* and love performing the solo couple in the Mazurka which I dance at every performance. I feel restless, however. It must be the spring.

May 16th 1984

Cramp and stomach ache woke me this morning due, I suspect, to nerves at the prospect of a rehearsal with the Russian choreographer Valery Panov. I had dared to ask him to coach me in Olga's solo from his ballet *Three Sisters*. He was inspirational to work with, giving no foundation for my anxieties. He approved of my feeling, "I can see you have lots of temperament" he told me, but worked to get my body expressing the emotions more clearly. He encouraged me to make the most of my femininity; opening my shoulders and turnout muscles in my thighs to their maximum. My back was made to stretch more and my legs needed to reach beyond their extensions. He wanted the movements to be expansive and dramatic and pulled my body into contortions like I do with my sculptures, whilst telling me to "devour the space".

Gradually I'm getting costumes and recordings organised for the competition, but it involves endlessly chasing people to get things done.

This week is full, with seven performances in eight days of three different programmes, and a Dutch aunt is staying with me. It's lovely to have a visitor, but I'm too busy to fully enjoy her company.

May 28th 1984

Class was interrupted today for a union meeting and representatives of the dancers informed the company of the Opera director's unsavoury plans for the Ballet company. These include no increase in wages (which are already considerably lower than the orchestra or opera chorus), a reduction in ballet performances, and a reduction in dancers to a company of about thirty. Everyone was furious of course and after a long discussion it was decided to take immediate action. Thus there was a sit down strike during rehearsals and the press were informed. The protest was announced to the audience at this evening's performance.

Marina Stavitskaya from Leningrad in Russia, now living in New York, is our current guest teacher and is coaching me in my competition solos. I like working with her and it's nice to have a feminine touch in my coaching as I have been working with male teachers.

News of John Field's resignation makes my chances of getting into Festival Ballet more difficult again. Everything seems so uncertain everywhere ...

June 8th 1984

The electric atmosphere in the company has cooled down now Egon Madsen is here and is negotiating with the Opera director for us.

These long summer days are evocative of the atmosphere in Strindberg's play, and Birigit Culberg's ballet, *Miss Julie*. I can well imagine how the heroine would behave at a Midsummer's party with the intoxication of energetic festivities during a night which doesn't get dark. I find it difficult to sleep and am restless. It gets dark after 11pm and dawn has broken by 3am. The long hours of daylight are as strange to me as those of darkness in the winter.

June 13th 1984

The season ended with the ballet company's annual "spring" party. At one point some dancers performed a short cabaret with hilarious skits about the company. There was a lot of food and dancing. It was great fun and for the first time since I arrived here I experienced a real sense of belonging.

Now I have two weeks left before I go to Helsinki. I attend classes in the morning at the Ballet Academy and rehearse my solos in the afternoon. A dancer friend is being my "eyes", watching the rehearsals and giving observations, helping me to produce myself in the final stages of preparation. The costumes are almost ready. I'm making my headdress and arm bands for *Raymonda*. I use the studios at the Opera House to work, and have a key to get into a studio at Midsummer when everything will be shut for four days. They take Midsummer more seriously than Christmas here.

June 23rd 1984

So much nervous, excited anticipation … It was good to have a break from packing and darning pointe shoes yesterday when Alex persuaded me to go out for dinner with him. He has offered to drive me to the Port of Stockholm, from where I'll take the boat to Helsinki, which I gladly accept as I'll be weighed down with costumes and bags.

I'm looking forward to my holiday after the competition. I'll make use of the Eurorail pass I bought and travel by train to Holland and then on to Switzerland where I'll meet my parents. I am so impatient to sit by the lake and watch the sunset illuminating the mountains opposite.

Chapter Six

Helsinki 1984

June 24th 1984

I am not a superstitious person but when the clouds break and the sun shines after a weekend of rain just in time to brighten my trip through the Stockholm archipelago en route for Helsinki, I feel convinced it marks the beginning of an exciting adventure. Sitting in a bar on the Viking Song ferry I watch the green islands glide past. So many times this year I have sailed this route through emeralds in a satin sea, and dreamed of the time I would journey further into the Baltic Sea to the far shores of Finland. Now after months of preparations I am really on my way. My costumes which I worked so hard to organise, are hanging in my cabin downstairs and I hope they won't be creased when I unpack them tomorrow.

June 25th 1984

I can see the dome of Helsinki's much photographed cathedral rising on the horizon, so I know we shall soon be arriving. My emotion is suspended in a knot of anticipation in the pit of my stomach.

Later, I am sitting alone in room 797 of the very large, rather impersonal Hotel President; no sign of a roommate yet. I already feel exhausted and nauseated from excitement and I know I am going to have to calm myself down and take control of my nerves.

Everything here seems wonderfully well organised. I was met by representatives from the competition who drove me to the hotel. I was greeted by a pile of information leaflets in my room about the city and the competition. There is free transport to and from the city centre, coupons for meals, sightseeing tours and invitations to receptions. I feel as if I am taking part in an international conference rather than a ballet competition.

To my surprise, the first thing I asked for was a studio to work in. Did I really imagine I was going to spend today sightseeing? Time enough for that later on. Now there is work to be done if I want to produce a decent performance for the first round.

Rehearsal studios scattered around Helsinki are at the disposal of competitors and I was taken to one by a Finnish voluntary helper who has offered to look after the British team, as she is an Anglophile. It turns out

124

that I am the only British competitor. She is a charming young woman and her English is impeccable. She tells me how she has done this job for athletic and skating events before. In fact, she looked after Torvill and Dean when they won the World Championship in Helsinki last year. So of course I feel I'm in very good company with her, and am inspired by her associations with two of my favourite ice skaters.

My rehearsal felt strange, alone in an unfamiliar studio. The floor was slippery and sounded hollow, echoing my pointe shoes every time I jumped. Nonetheless, I felt I achieved something and was grateful to have a studio to work in at all.

A bus took those of us who wanted to go, to the opening of an exhibition at the City Theatre about "Les Ballets Suédois"; a movement in the 1920s of a group of dancers who broke away from the Royal Opera in Stockholm to create new experimental work in Europe and America. Their choreographer Jean Börlin was only a young man and burned himself out creating twenty-four new works in four years. Afterwards he had a break down and died a few years later, only in his thirties. There was a fascinating display of costumes and set designs and the director of the Dance Museum of Stockholm, Bengt Häger, gave an engaging lecture.

After this, there was the drawing of lots. Everyone sat in the auditorium and then contestants were called to the stage in order of nationality to draw their number. Faces were long if the number was low and smiling if it was high. The latter are more popular as this means a couple of extra days to rehearse before presenting oneself and less time to wait for the results. My number is sixty-six so I expect to dance on the third and last day of the first round. There are about seventy competitors.

As I was leaving the stage, I was ushered to the side to be interviewed by Finnish television. This was most unexpected and I felt my legs turn to jelly. I was asked why I am the only British competitor, which was a difficult question to answer. I suggested that perhaps the dancers in England work too hard to have time for competitions. I was also asked what I thought of my number and whether it's better to be at the beginning or the end. All I could reply was that one wants to do one's best whenever one is on. The observation was made that I am dancing in Sweden and the interviewer asked if I feel I am representing Sweden or Britain. So, feeling patriotic, I said Britain because I was trained there.

Seeking refuge back in my room after dinner at the theatre canteen, I am delighted and relieved to find that I still have it all to myself. I rather hope I'll be lucky and keep my privacy.

125

June 26th 1984

The day began for me with the abrupt beeps of my alarm clock. I was bewildered to awaken in my Helsinki hotel room. Once I'd dressed, my first move was downstairs to investigate the day's schedule on the notice board. I saw that there was a class at nine each morning at the theatre with Rimma Karelskaya from the Bolshoi Ballet, and that I'd been given a rehearsal slot in one of the other studios afterwards today.

I was very curious to sample a Bolshoi class. It was fast and uncomplicated. We were perspiring heavily after the twenty minutes of barre work, and a whole half hour was given to allegro (jumps), which I enjoyed. The lively inspiring music by the pianist was a great bonus. I was too involved in my own work to watch critically, but I was aware of some very talented young men. There must have been about three quarters of the competitors in the class and the studio was large enough to accommodate all of us. It seems that some of the dancers have come in teams and work only with their own coaches, such as the Russians, for example. Eyebrows are raised when I admit to not having a coach with me. There was quite a large audience of teachers and friends sitting at the back of the studio and I found this stimulating; so much better than the complacency and monotony that can dominate regular company classes.

After my rehearsal I took advantage of the physiotherapy facilities on offer to competitors, and a relaxing massage helped relieve the knots in my shoulders from carrying my heavy luggage and costumes.

All the facilities at the theatre are modern, spacious and functional. The stage is large and although the auditorium seats nine hundred, it has an intimate feel. Dressing rooms have been allocated to everyone and I am sharing with two Romanian girls.

This afternoon I wandered through the town, passing the waterfront market and tree lined avenues. I found my way through a maze-like shopping complex ending up in one of the main shopping streets, Aleksanterinkatu. Window shopping the whole way down the street I arrived at the very impressive and elegant Senaatintori (Senate Square) on which Helsinki's lovely cathedral gazes down in white serenity. The desire to see inside was great enough to motivate me to climb the steep steps and the effort was well worthwhile. I found the predominance of white walls and wooden seats purifying.

The air is very fresh here, even more invigorating than Stockholm. However, the locals don't all seem to think so, and I get curious looks from people as I half skip down the streets not attempting to conceal a spontaneous smile from my face. There seem to be more drunks here than in Stockholm and generally people do not look happy.

The reception this evening was a grand affair. Three bus loads of people representing the competition left the hotel. The evening was well organised: speeches were brief, there was a charming display of folk dancing, and a variety of food and drinks. I was grateful to be chaperoned by my Finnish volunteer helper, always faithfully by my side. People are even beginning to comment on my private guide service! I suppose I must be a bit of an oddity to the young man who introduced himself to me as a member of the American contingent. I confidently assured him that I am the British contingent! He seemed to find it slightly outrageous that I don't have an entourage with me.

Reading a copy of the competition programme, it is interesting to find out about the other dancers and the judges. There is obviously a lot of talent and quite a few of the competitors have already won important prizes at other competitions.

After all the buzz of the day, I was thankful to find the other bed in my room still unoccupied. I do hope it stays that way.

June 27th 1984

Waiting…waiting…waiting…this is the worst, and I have a tangle of nerves in my stomach most of the time. I shall perform in two days. My body feels broken and it took tremendous discipline to force myself to work today. This afternoon there was a short bus tour of Helsinki and a rehearsal for the opening ceremony this evening.

Once the opening ceremony was over there was a two and a half hour nonstop marathon of variations and pas de deux. Standards are mixed, but there is a lot of talent. At first, I was nervous watching the dancers onstage knowing that in two days time it will be my turn. I started to relax as I enjoyed the dancing of some very talented Russians and Finns. The Japanese juniors stood out, and a little Romanian girl who is sharing my dressing room stole everyone's hearts, including mine. The audience is frighteningly attentive, but eager to cheer and applaud the performers.

June 28th 1984

There is little to do today except organise practicalities of costumes, shoes and so on, and to organise my brain and emotions as best I can into a state of calm confidence. I have been able to see the lighting options and chose the best available for my variations.

I am still very hyped up and tense inside. There is a confusion of excitement at what could happen at best, fear of what could happen at worst, concern to make the most of every second I hold the stage, and a general impatience to get going. So much has happened already and I've lived every moment so intensely, scarcely getting any sleep. It's hard to believe this is only the fourth day. I keep telling myself it will be a relief when the first round is over, but I know it won't really, unless I'm eliminated. This would inevitably sting my pride, but I daresay I could adjust myself to a holiday in Helsinki as all competitors are invited to remain until the end of the contest, regardless of how far they get in it.

Preparing myself for performance is no vacation. Quite apart from practice, my schedule involves taking care of my body: hot baths, massage, ice to reduce the swelling of my sore muscles. I'm improvising ice packs from ice cubes available for drinks in a refrigerator on each landing of the hotel and plastic bags. As long as the bags don't leak it is effective. It's no fun being hungry all the time either. It must be nerves and lack of sleep that make me constantly hungry. But if I give in to the pangs and eat everything I desire, I'll soon lose my relatively sylph-like outline.

It came as a blow to be told this afternoon that as I'm in a twin room on my own, I should move into a room with someone else who is alone. I contacted the girl I was supposed to share with, who was very nervous as she was performing tonight, and she found the idea of sharing as upsetting as I did. In the end the solution was to stay in our rooms on our own at an extra cost. It took just a few seconds for both of us to make the adjustment to parting with the money rather than losing our privacy. It occurred to me that even the smallest prize would pay my hotel bill, whereupon I found my first incentive to win one.

There was another reception today given by the city of Helsinki at the City Hall. This grand building is modern and spacious with an elegantly decorated reception hall. I was surprised that so few people attended. There were mostly judges, attachés and organisers. I only saw one other dancer. The huge hall seemed empty and the plentiful food and wine remained almost neglected, except for the slices of yellow pepper which I attacked with relish. I was thankful to have my voluntary helper at my side. We have coffees and lunches together sometimes, and she is becoming a friend.

I met the British judge, Alexander Grant, who congratulated me on my courage in entering this competition. It is rare for a British dancer to participate in an international competition. Nationalities of the competitors here are dominated by East Europeans, Americans and Japanese. The former take these contests very seriously as an opportunity to expose themselves to international criticism, and they are given considerable help by their teachers and directors in presenting themselves.

The day concluded with another barrage of *Don Quixote* and *Le Corsaire* pas de deux and variations. Despite the wide choice of repertoire, these are by far the most popular show pieces. Standards range from brilliant to appalling, and in general the men outshine the women. Tomorrow it will be my turn and I'm looking forward to the few moments which will be mine. I feel the audience is really warming up. They always applaud politely, but take an opportunity to show more appreciation too. I wonder how they will react to me, and how I shall react to them. I realise that this is an especially attentive audience which wants very much to applaud the dancers. Judging by the standard, I think there is a chance I could pass to the second round. We shall see …

June 29th 1984

I slept badly again the night before my turn to perform, nerves grabbing hold of me. There was a good class with Rimma Karelskaya in the morning with plenty of room to move as it was poorly attended. Then I had a stage rehearsal which gave me the opportunity to orientate myself. It was so much more satisfying to dance to the black auditorium, even though it was empty, than to practise in front of the mirror reflecting all my faults. I spent the afternoon resting; no sightseeing today.

It is a relief to have this evening's performance behind me now. Some tension was released in the show and that helped calm me down a little. *Raymonda* went well. There are details I could improve on (there always are), but the flow was good and the technique was strong. I received a warm spontaneous applause and someone gave me a "bravo". *Giselle* was not so good. I felt it was uneven, some parts technically secure, some less so. I think I maintained the style and freshness and the applause, though less enthusiastic than for the first solo, was warm nonetheless. I was angry with myself about *Giselle*, but there's nothing I can do about it now. I think I achieved the effect I'd intended; establishing a rapport with the audience and showing a range of style and quality to the judges. I don't know if it's enough to go through to round two. I may have a chance, not because I am particularly good, but because the other girls are generally not so brilliant. It is still the boys who are shining. Whatever happens to me, I shall be curious to see how those talented boys progress through the rounds.

Now I'm looking forward to soaking in a hot bath and washing my hair. By the time I've finished pampering myself I might creep downstairs and see if the results have been announced.

June 30th 1984

When the results of the first round were pinned on the board at 1.30am this morning, I saw that I have passed to the second round. I'm very pleased about this as it gives me the opportunity to present *Birdsong*. I'll have to concentrate on rehearsing my programme for the finals now just in case I pass through to the third round. However, today I could afford to give myself a day off and relax on a trip to Haikko which was arranged for us. The advantage of feeling exhausted today is that I no longer have the energy to be nervous, and at last the knot in my stomach has melted away.

The drive through the rolling woodland, similar to the Swedish landscape, took us to the beautiful Haikko Manor set in lovely grounds, which is now a hotel and health resort. In the gardens I found a small exhibition including work by the artist Laila Pullinen who has designed the competition posters and award sculpture. Her work is striking and the sculptures are full of movement and fantasy. After a buffet lunch there was a boat trip along the coast back to Helsinki.

July 1st 1984

After class and rehearsal this morning, I decided to make use of my Eurorail pass and visit the home of the composer Jean Sibelius in Järvenpää some miles north of Helsinki. There was drizzle as I walked the two and a half kilometres from the station to the house, and the bleak atmosphere of the surrounding countryside reminded me of Sibelius' evocative music. When I finally arrived, I found the house, Ainola, placed in the middle of a wood, to be very cosy and I imagine he must have been peacefully contented here. The Finns are proud of their famous composer as they demonstrate with their imposing monument dedicated to him in Helsinki.

The first session of the second round was a disappointment. I found most of the choreography to be poor and the dancers were seldom shown to advantage. My solo will stand up well against the pieces tonight, but there are still two nights to go as well as the finals. It finished early with each dancer performing just once and I was relieved not to have to sit through so many repetitious pieces as during the first round.

July 2nd 1984

I feel fairly calm now and able to relax better; just impatient to show my choreography and get some feedback. There have been daily reviews in the local newspapers of the competition and I was mentioned for my *Raymonda*, something on the lines of: it was a refreshing change (I was the only person to choose this variation), and mention of my elegance and sophistication.

My stage rehearsal this morning went smoothly. Everyone seems to have chosen such complicated, virtuosic numbers. I feel like a cheat, doing something so relatively easy. The challenge is in remaining calm and composed.

July 3rd 1984

Waiting ... a lot of waiting...but at last I performed *Birdsong* this evening which was received with intense concentration from the audience and warm applause calling me back three times to bow. It felt extraordinarily easy, and I had to concentrate not to be distracted. My confidence was perhaps inappropriate as I have not passed to the third round. Many people expressed their appreciation of *Birdsong* and this is tremendously satisfying.

The results of the second round have been received with obvious disapproval from many sides. Not everyone agrees with the judges' decisions and several people told me they thought I should have gone through. The results do look suspiciously political to me, especially where the Finns are concerned. Very few of these have been eliminated, at the expense of some very talented dancers of other nationalities. Most of the finalists are showing their work with a partner rather than solos. Dancers presenting themselves individually, like me, would seem to be at a disadvantage.

I am disappointed not to have the chance to perform the last three variations I have spent months preparing. On the other hand, the pressure is off me now and I can relax and enjoy the last few days.

July 4th 1984

I couldn't sleep last night and went to the cafeteria in the hotel. A group of Czech girls were sitting there indulging in some enormous ice creams. I can imagine the disappointment of one of them who has been eliminated even though she has been a prize winner several times before at other competitions. I can also understand the sense of relief and rebellion allowing them to gobble ice cream so freely in the early hours of the morning. Later I enjoyed the biggest breakfast I've eaten in ages.

In my customary way, as soon as one thing is over, I am impatient to commence the next. In this case, it is my holiday and my mind is running circles planning it all. For a start I have the next three days to plan.

Today's sightseeing was organised for me, another for the people involved in the competition. It was a lovely sunny day and I caught glimpses of the passing scenery between my fluttering eyelids as I tried not to drop off to sleep during the long coach ride. The countryside is very rich after the recent rain, vivid greens and yellows. Perhaps the pure, clean air here heightens the images. The countryside is natural and unspoilt, quite a paradise, with endless undulating forests dotted with the occasional effervescent red or yellow wooden stuga (cottage).

First stop was at a glass museum where we were greeted with champagne and a superb display of famous Finnish glassware. Then the bus took us to the town of Hämeenlinna one hundred kilometres north of Helsinki. It was the birthplace of Sibelius and here, as in many other towns, can be found museums, monuments and streets bearing his name. We were received at the Art Gallery; more alcoholic refreshment and a brief viewing of the exhibits. Some Finnish paintings with a real fairytale quality captured my imagination. Time for lunch and we were driven to the luxurious Hotel Aulanko situated in a beautiful park with panoramic views over neighbouring lakes. A guided bus tour of Hämeenlinna concluded with a tour of the medieval castle.

The return journey was broken up with a stop at Rajamäki where a buffet dinner awaited us on the lawn of a charming country house. A visit to a typical old Finnish farmhouse and the museum of a vodka factory concluded a long but satisfying day.

The conversations I had were as enlightening as the sightseeing. Over lunch I spoke with a Japanese man who told me how hard it is for dancers in Japan who are unable to have full-time contracts because dance is not government supported. He almost turned green when I told him of the comfort and security enjoyed by the dancers in Sweden. An American journalist was dubious about the whole idea of ballet competitions. After all, how can one judge Art? She also disagreed with some of the jury's decisions. Similar thoughts were echoed by an English dance writer who suggested that competitions are not the only thing in the ballet world to be influenced by internal politics rather than quality and worth. He thinks that there is no place for the really sensitive person in the Ballet world and an enormous amount of talent is wasted because of this. Being in the right place at the right time is essential, and in his opinion the only way to find any happiness in this profession is not to be too ambitious, but to work for yourself because you want to, which he suggested is rather what I am doing. He also told of intrigues and how "political" the workings of a ballet company are. According to him, Artistic Directors are pawns to be manipulated by everyone. These thoughts ring true in my ears. I don't like to hear them because I like to believe in good and justice, and reward for achievement. But in my heart of hearts I know the latter is a coincidence, not a fact.

Many people praised *Birdsong* including several of the judges who participated in the excursion. Alexander Grant told me I performed with "great style". Doris Laine (the Finnish judge) said she didn't recognise me because I've lost so much weight; we met before, during my "fat" Düsseldorf days. Jeanne Brabants (the judge from Belgium) asked me how I knew so much about birds; a lifetime of observation.

July 5th 1984

This morning when I went to class, although it felt good to move and perspire, somehow I couldn't take the work seriously. My concentration was the minimum necessary not to make a fool of myself or injure myself. It just didn't matter anymore if my pirouettes worked or not. I enjoyed the sensation of moving for its own sake.

After the busy day of tourism yesterday, I had a quieter day today, walking around Helsinki. The novelty of the city has worn off now and I find a lot of it to be a drab town filled by generally miserable looking people.

I arrived back in my hotel room later to see an excerpt from the second round of the ballet competition on television. Part of *Birdsong* was shown. I didn't understand a word of the commentary, but it was rather thrilling to see myself on television. I was displeased by my dancing; it had felt better than it looked. I promised myself to improve my next performance, whenever that might be. Perhaps I was just in a critical mood because I was disappointed with the first session of the finals. I had expected everyone to be pulling out all the stops, but in fact most were nervous and making mistakes. I regret just a tiny bit that I'm denied the opportunity to perform my other three variations. However, it was part of the deal to prepare them knowing that I might not get a chance to show them. There are plenty of people more disappointed than me. On the other hand, it is actually quite a relief not to have the tension anymore.

July 6th 1984

A smooth comfortable train took me on the three hour trip to Turku today as I took advantage of my rail pass again. Finnish trains are even cleaner and more efficient than Swedish ones. A far cry from the stuffy London commuter trains. The carriages are spacious and modern. The only difference between first and second class seems to be the colour of the seats.

I was so glad to have this opportunity to make a longer journey in Finland on my own, and to escape the competition atmosphere where there is now a lot bickering, bitterness and criticism.

In under four hours I was able to see a lot and it was a pleasure to walk around the town in the sunshine. Distances were further than I'd anticipated from the little map in my Berlitz guide, but I still managed to do everything I'd planned.

I began with the cathedral which is apparently the Finnish equivalent to England's Westminster Abbey. It was worth seeing, but not to my taste. I much prefer Helsinki's cathedral for the purity of its style. Nearby I found another Sibelius museum. There was little about the composer, but a magnificent collection of musical instruments.

More walking and I arrived at the Handicrafts museum which consists of original old cottages where all kinds of craftsmen and women lived and worked. It is similar to Skansen in Stockholm, only smaller and more concentrated. The weaver, lace maker, carpenter, potter, even a stained glass maker, could all be found here. The big surprise was to discover a violin maker's workshop with old cramps, chisels and planes, wood stacked high on shelves, violin fronts and backs in preparation and re-serves of bow hair hanging up. It was all there, even the melting pots for the varnish. The neighbouring bedroom contained a music stand for the luthier to practise. It reminded me of my father who, in his retirement, has started combining his woodwork and musical skills to make stringed instruments. I felt very close to him at that moment and missed him dreadfully.

I returned to the station via the market place and the orthodox church which were both more attractive in the travel brochures than in reality. I fell asleep on the train back to Helsinki and arrived just in time to watch the second evening of the final round. I am very tired now, having made a decision on a plan of action, I simply followed it without another thought. I had sufficient energy to propel myself through my schedule. My emotions are dulled and being busy, without pressure, rescued me from falling into a deflated depression.

July 7th 1984

What a way to wake up! I crawled out of bed early to check if there was class this morning and my eye passed to the rehearsal list for the awards gala this evening. This gave an indication of who the prize winners would be, although the official announcement was not made until this evening. After watching the finals I was as curious as everyone else to know how the awards would be distributed. To my shock I saw my name on the list for a rehearsal of *Birdsong*. It was only much later, after the results were announced secretly to the press, that I persuaded a journalist to tell me my position. I discovered that I'd been awarded the third prize for choreography.

It took all I had to pull myself together for that performance. I had no energy left to be nervous and had to work hard to maintain concentration. So many people congratulated me afterwards that now I am filled with their warmth, but the moment before I stepped onstage was one of the loneliest of my life. I felt no inspiration, no desire to dance, just emptiness and total aloneness. It was the most terrible, desolate feeling. Whatever reserves of Art and professionalism I have were drawn on for that performance. It was a struggle. Last time it had been so easy, but who knows which is better. I again received a very warm response from the audience. Applause started before the lights had faded out and I was called back three times to enthusiastic cheers. In the wings I burst into floods of tears, all the emotions of the last two weeks gushing forth.

Positive feedback is encouraging and several judges took the trouble to speak to me personally. Robert Joffrey was especially warm and encouraged me to continue choreographing. His suggestion that my ballet technique needs strengthening was meant as kind advice, but was disappointing for me to hear. I work so hard at my wretched body, will I ever achieve the fashionable virtuoso technique? Alexander Grant was chuffed that I won a prize and demonstrated that "the British can be unconventional".

Several people commented that they enjoyed a second viewing of *Birdsong*. It was particularly satisfying to hear one lady tell me that it had converted her to contemporary dance, after only appreciating classical ballet before. A Swedish man congratulated me saying that the only thing wrong with me is that I am not Swedish!

July 8th 1984

I spent today waiting, yet again, this time to leave Helsinki. It was a glorious day and I spent a lot of it scoffing ice cream.

Looking back on the competition, by the time it came to the finals, some dancers were looking very strained, whilst others managed to look confident and relaxed. Of course there was a lot of discussion about the results and most of the Finnish people I spoke to thought that the abundance of awards to Finns was a little exaggerated. Everyone was glad the French couple did well. The gala was a glitzy event, for the audience anyway. Most of the dancers were exhausted but glad it was all over, especially those who had won prizes. It was a less joyous occasion for those who were eliminated after the second round but had to continue to partner finalists. Dancers were judged on individual merits, even when competing in a partnership.

Finally, I said goodbye to my Finnish volunteer helper promising to exchange letters as I boarded my boat.

Suddenly I feel very rich, even after paying my hotel bill I have several hundred pounds of prize money in cash in my purse. I don't know what I'll do with it. Somehow it feels unreal, like play money. It's so far removed from the essence of the competition.

I sit in a trance, suspended in limbo in the television lounge. Before me on the screen I watch dancing figures from the competition which I saw recently at the Helsinki City Theatre. The image blurs as reception from Finland fades with the passing kilometres and my memories become hazy like a forgotten dream. Did it all really happen?

Chapter Seven

Stockholm   Part Two

1984 - 1986

August 15th 1984

News of my victory in Helsinki reached Sweden and many people congratulated me. The competition was reviewed in the newspapers here. I felt relieved rather than victorious when it was all over, and after the gala I ate only ice cream for a whole day in rebellion against the strict discipline I normally impose on myself.

Starting my summer holiday, I travelled south by train and spent some hours in Copenhagen, a city which had captured my imagination when I passed through before. I found myself visiting the zoo as most of the museums were shut that day. It was here that I watched a wonderful collection of exotic birds in an aviary including one particular specimen with a very haughty, elegant gait so strongly reminiscent of *Birdsong* that I found myself exclaiming out loud: "Hey! You've stolen my choreography!"

Continuing my journey I went to Holland, and in a whirl of excitement saw my friends and relatives. I had liked Copenhagen so much that I used my rail pass to return again from Amsterdam, taking the sleeper train there and back, giving me a whole day to explore. When I took a canal trip from the colourful Nyhaven, I noticed the ferry to Malmö in Sweden. Not satisfied with just one town, and realising that my rail pass gave me a reduction on the ferries, I hopped on one for a quick excursion to Malmö.

I was still hyped up when I met my parents in Switzerland and found it extremely difficult to unwind, both mentally and physically. I was possessed with an abundance of restless energy, riding high on my recent success. My father was going through an exceptionally bad period with his health. At first I didn't realise because I was so preoccupied with myself, and my lack of sensitivity towards him only exasperated his condition. When I finally became aware of what was happening, I was very frightened, both for his survival and for my humanity. I blamed my extreme self-involvement on the demands my ambitions made on my body, mind and soul. How was I going to find a compromise: to be a dancer and a compassionate human being? I returned to Stockholm with very mixed feelings.

Egon Madsen has taken up his post as ballet director and his wife, Lucia Isenring, is here as a soloist. She is a superb dancer and artist; an example for us all. Rehearsals revolve around preparing for the tour to Lapland with *Swan Lake* and *Nutcracker*. There is nothing new for me to learn. I try to give myself fresh challenges by experimenting with my choreography and have started another solo. I have a lot of free time and spend much of it being massaged out of the knots I get my muscles into.

August 25th 1984

The discovery that I am to learn the role of Olga in *Three Sisters* has cheered me out of a depression. This is a role which requires sensitivity and drama rather than technical fireworks. I already know her main solo as I prepared it for Helsinki. I sympathise totally with Olga's desire to escape Moscow; like mine to leave Stockholm and return to England. I'm reading Chekov's play again and analysing all the characters. It is wonderful to be involved in something new and I hope so much for a chance to perform Olga.

However, homesickness gnaws at me and I'm concerned about my father. I am so far away if he needs me. Alex is on holiday for four weeks and I miss him too. It's comforting when I know he is around and I can phone him for a chat.

September 3rd 1984

I am learning the role of Olga from the video and working on it on my own, as rehearsals for *Three Sisters* have not started yet. I'm so impatient to work ...

September 9th 1984

My dreams suggest disturbance in my subconscious. They range from the violent to the erotic, associations with home and working with different companies. Deep inside I fear uprooting and moving again even though I often consider it. The idea of moving to another company keeps me on my toes, so to speak. It stops me from drifting into comfortable lethargy. I would like to feel more settled here and yet I seem unable to do so. Perhaps sometime I will reach a certain degree of maturity when I will have learned to live with myself in tranquility. I am always striving for this, but seldom seem to achieve it for long. I recognise that I shall never "arrive", for life is always in motion. But it must be possible to attain a level of stability within oneself from which to move forwards in life, instead of constantly going round in circles. I feel I am not formed yet; I get bounced about by the waves of life. The insecurity of my job makes me feel rootless. Perhaps I need more involvement in my work than I have at present, or perhaps I shall have to stop dancing to find this solid thing I'm searching for. The dancing itself is so precarious and unpredictable.

September 15th 1984

Rehearsals for *Three Sisters* have started at last. A soloist and myself are learning the part of Olga and there seems to be a chance that one of us will perform it. The principal who usually dances it will be away for a couple of performances, and the second cast Olga is injured. The other girl is exceptionally tall and I would certainly look better with the other two "sisters". She shows absolutely no enthusiasm for the part and is slow to learn it, which is beyond my comprehension. It seems reasonable to presume I have a chance to dance Olga, there is even a costume for me which I took to Helsinki. But no matter how keen and determined I may be, I am in competition with an established, Swedish, soloist. We shall wait to see the outcome, but I can't help hoping.

We performed today at an enormous sports hall in Handen close to Stockholm. Travelling here by coach with the company reminded me of days with Scapino Ballet, in a cosy way.

A bad cold is tiring me. The dreaded germ has a tendency to strike when I lose weight and I have been trying to diet after gaining a kilo over the holidays. It seems especially difficult because my periods have returned, unsettling my emotions even more than usual.

September 23rd 1984

It's nice to be back in Stockholm after a few days in Västerås, which is about two hours drive away. Four performances of *Nutcracker* in three days made a hectic schedule. Waltz of the Flowers in Spoerli's version is a technical feat to accomplish and I still get nervous for it sometimes. No-one likes doing it very much, but apparently it looks good from the audience. The constant motion of the pale pink and peach dresses is like rose petals blowing in the wind. A new means of inspiration I discovered was to sing to myself whilst dancing. This helped my flow of movement and distracted me from the difficult steps. I am first cast for the Arabian dance now and always enjoy this.

Västerås is a pleasant town with, I thought, a slightly Finnish rather than Swedish character. The church in particular reminded me of one I had seen in Finland. I also liked the little canal surrounded by colourful wooden houses and trees.

Alex has returned and it was nice to see him before we leave for the tour to Lapland.

September 27th 1984

It looked like Christmas when we were greeted by a carpet of snow and freezing temperatures as we landed at Kiruna above the arctic circle. My first view of Lapland was of snow tipped peaks rising above the low fluffy clouds. On arrival the mountains were not visible at ground level, but later the weather cleared to reveal a stunning view of them from the town. It was strange to fly for an hour and a half and not leave Sweden. It is a larger country than one realises. The cold weather was a shock, but we had been warned to take warm clothes with us. Once I started to acclimatise, I found the tangy freshness of the air revitalising.

Kiruna feels like a different country from the South of Sweden. The life pulse of Kiruna is the iron ore mine and we were taken on a guided tour. I hated it! It was cold, damp and dark, and all I wanted to do was get out again. Even so, it was an opportunity not to be missed. My favourite sight in Kiruna is the church which looks magical in the snow with its fairytale quality and simple, rustic style. The Lapps have a stockier build, speak with a dialect I hardly understand, and have their own culture and traditions. They very seldom have the chance to see live performances and receive us with tremendous warmth and standing ovations.

September 29th 1984

The Arabian dance was cheered this evening, and the principals were not! This made the "Arabians" glow with pride. I am recognised as a dancer in the street and get asked to sign my autograph. We are local celebrities in this small community: a change from Stockholm where we get taken for granted.

September 30th 1984

Picture postcard vistas pass before my eyes through the train window. What a thrill to discover new scenery and watch the travel brochures come to life. Leaving the flat barren landscape of Kiruna with snow capped mountains in the distance, we pass through lakeland and undulating hills as the colours become vivid yellows and browns. Moving into Norwegian Lapland the land is barren and desolate, but enveloped in a mystical atmosphere. The route follows a gorge with the train track becoming increasingly narrow and passing through a very rocky area. Approaching Narvik, the destination, the view becomes even more dramatic with a deep fjord diving below. This is the Ofotfjord which leads out to the sea and Narvik, which is also a port, is the main town in the area.

On the three-hour train journey I eavesdrop on a conversation between a local man and some visitors to the area. He is on his way into the hills to hunt wild fowl and deer, and looks dressed for the occasion. He points out a group of mountains, known as the gate of Lapland, claiming to have climbed them many times. Then he talks about the difficulty of living with the climate in the region with the very long, very dark, very cold winter: three months of darkness. Then there is the extreme opposite in the summer with three months of daylight. Apparently, people here suffer from "Lapp sickness". I can well imagine.

In Narvik I take the cable car up the mountain with a company pianist who is my companion on this trip and we are rewarded with stunning panoramic views over the mountains and the bay below gleaming in the sunshine.

I am very tired and return early to snowy Kiruna where a thick fog is descending, well satisfied with the excursion.

October 3rd 1984

Over three hundred kilometres bus ride through almost uninhabited hilly forests, lakes and rivers and we pass through just two towns between Kiruna and Luleå. It is autumn here rather than winter and the verdure of the evergreens is streaked with brilliant golds and flame orange autumn leaves which still dress the birch tree branches. These bright colours are a dramatic contrast against the silver grey sky. Some rain is welcome. It indicates temperatures too high for snow, and I hope my frozen toes will now thaw out. Again, we are staying in a first class hotel and I have a room to myself. Here we shall perform *Swan Lake*.

October 6th 1984

Our director Egon joins us in Luleå and brings a feeling of coherence. The company has more respect for him than our other ballet staff who struggle sometimes to maintain authority. Audiences are more reserved than in Kiruna, perhaps reflecting the heaviness of the grey mist which is enveloping the town. One of our dancers originates from Luleå and organises a fun party for the whole company. He admits that this region is often foggy and rainy. He too can be quite sulky.

I am able to chat with various people at breakfast, and sharing dressing rooms with different dancers from usual helps me get to know my colleagues a little better. Mostly I find myself commiserating with the other foreigners about how difficult it is to communicate with the Swedes. Mia and her family are the only Swedish people I have been able to form a friendship with. I am certainly very thankful for that. It's a shame that my cousin Steve is no longer flying to Stockholm.

The final performance of *Swan Lake* sees many jokes onstage, taking advantage of the absence of the director who has now returned to Stockholm. My favourite is an agreement between all the swans in Act Two, apart from two brave ones who remain on the stage, to elegantly vacate the stage for the pas de deux and variations. What a relief not to have to stand in the poses on the side getting cramp! We all reappear in time for the final coda. In the Mazurka in Act Three we girls wear the men's hats. The princesses in this act who try to attract the prince's attention come in donning beauty contest sashes announcing the country they represent; "Miss Italy" etc. These are swiftly removed before their dance starts. I suggest to the ballerina dancing the role of "Odile" that she wears one saying "Miss World". She thinks this is a great idea, but there isn't enough time in the choreography to remove it before the Black Swan pas de deux. The best part however, must be when the swans make their entrance in Act Two from one side of the stage and the boys stand in the wings on the other side and drop their trousers to reveal all! Unfortunately, I miss the display because I am at the front and too concentrated, but it must be highly distracting for the girls who see it. Needless to say, I'm very annoyed that I miss it!

October 10th 1984

Back in Stockholm, it is a relief to be in my flat again. It was strenuous in Luleå rehearsing *Three Sisters* during the day and performing *Swan Lake* every night. I feel empty and deflated now. My isolation was emphasised when we arrived back at Stockholm's Arlanda airport and everyone seemed to have someone to meet them, or to go home with, except for me. I missed my father more than ever. I continue to worry about his health and ask myself if I am doing the right thing by being here.

Egon Madsen is definitely making his presence felt and I respect his artistic values very much. Future plans for the Royal Swedish Ballet are hazy as negotiations with the Opera director continue. Many of the dancers are sick or injured after the tour, and those who are not, are exhausted like me. It's so nice to come back to the comforts of the theatre studios after the draughty sports halls we have been dancing in. We are very spoilt in Stockholm.

Manon rehearsals are in progress now. I dance in the corps de ballet and cover a soloist part of a courtesan. This production by Kenneth MacMillan has long been one of my favourites so I'm delighted to be able to dance in it. I love the sense of period and history.

It occurs to me that I am in an awkward position in the company. As a relative newcomer (bearing in mind that the majority of dancers stay in this company for twenty years or more), a total outsider and quite an individual, I hover between the corps de ballet and the soloists. I sense a little envy from some of my colleagues in the group who wonder what is so special about me, and uncertainty from the senior dancers who do not know if I pose a threat or not. I would like to enjoy my work here and have friends in the company, but I am not sure where I fit in either. My lack of security and satisfaction in my private life lead me to cling to known elements such as work and books. It seems that the male dancers work it out so much better, trying out new steps and helping each other with jovial contests to see who can do the most pirouettes. There is always a frosty feeling amongst the women if one is the industrious type. One receives sideways glances as if to say "there's an ambitious one", as if it is a sin. In fact, I get on better with my male colleagues than my female ones.

October 14th 1984

Cast lists for *Three Sisters* inform us that I shall not dance the role of Olga. The other girl who was rehearsing the role with me will have two performances. I am dreadfully disappointed, but perhaps I should not have hoped for so much. She is an established soloist after all. Conversely, I experience a sense of relief at not having the pressure of responsibility. And I feel guilty about this. Where has my sense of ambition gone?

I'm very highly strung at the moment and frighten myself sometimes because I see the ultimate release from my suffering as death. Sometimes my energy is so low I just want to curl up and die. I know I'm tired, but it would be comforting to have a shoulder to cry on. I'm very resourceful, but how much longer can I hang on? Ever since the tour I seem to be in constant pain: knots in my back and hips. No amount of massage seems to help. A little alcohol helps me to relax in the evenings and only pain killers bring real relief. I am not injured. There is no logical explanation for the soreness.

143

October 16th 1984

I pour my confused emotions into the solo I am choreographing. I have chosen a costume from Jiri Kylian's *Ariadne* that I can use for it. Without music, it is aptly named *Silent Song*. The song should be in the flowing movements. Robert Browning's words, "Ah! But a man's reach should exceed his grasp or what's a heaven for?", are the starting point. I imagine the body being lit like a sculpture against a black velvety background. How I move will depend on where the movements take me and I imagine an energy force pulling me upwards - or maybe reaching upwards against gravity. An idea of striving, reaching to surpass the restrictions placed upon us by nature and society. There should be an intense atmosphere and my motivations for the movements are much more emotional than in *Birdsong*. It will perhaps be closer to my soul and personality, not so lightweight. I haven't decided how it will end: with submission to the downward force, or triumph against it, or a continuing turmoil of struggle left in limbo? It is fun not knowing where I'm going and watching the choreography grow.

October 22nd 1984

A male colleague has asked me to dance in his choreography for the next workshop. His style is fast and jazzy, and on pointe. It is a complete contrast from my controlled contemporary creations, and I am really enjoying the creative process with someone else.

November 1st 1984

I've taken my first day off from work since I've been in Sweden. It is total desperation and numbness of exhaustion which has prompted this. Premenstrual tension is causing a severe depression as well. Hopefully I can pull myself together if I relax today.

November 3rd 1984

I feel empty and lack purpose or inspiration. I have no ambition, which is a quality I dislike anyway. But worst of all I don't feel that I want to dance. And yet, when I do, I find it comes as a natural expression of things inside me which have to be released. It is hard for me to dance "professionally". Even in class I tend to take along my baggage of emotions of the moment and pour them out onto the dance studio floor. I suppose it's ok if it helps. I don't really know how it affects my dancing; I'm a poor judge of that. Keeping in contact with my inner self is very important to me, and dancing seems to help me to do this; even when I'm tired, in pain, or hating it. Well, I learned a long time ago to find masochistic satisfaction in the work. I think the fact that I am a dancer, regardless of ambitions or achievements, helps me. It offers an outlet for physical and emotional energy. That energy also involves physical contact with other human beings, and some emotional contact with them too. I don't know how many other jobs give one this. It's hard enough as it is, feeling so isolated and not having close loving friends or family, but I'd go quite crazy without the dancing.

November 6th 1984

My neighbour has hired a video recorder so I go next door to watch films with her, as well as television, on her large colour set. I'm very lucky to have her and I know I'm always welcome to drop in. I also appreciate Alex's friendship and the outings he sometimes takes me on in his car.

Rehearsals have started on a new piece by Uwe Scholz to be premiered in a triple bill in December. I am second cast for a solo part. The choreography is mostly very fast with a lot of pointe work for the women. I think Egon intends to strengthen the company's technique with this piece.

November 8th 1984

I'm still in the doldrums and lack a sense of purpose. The most tangible goal I have is the choreographic workshop at the end of January, but that is so far away. Uwe Scholz's ballet is definitely a challenge and we have no idea when the second cast will get a chance to perform it, if at all.

My weight is depressing as the needle is stuck at 51 kilos. I just cannot stick to a diet long enough to make any progress. It's hard to find motivation. I feel constantly frustrated because I am artistically under challenged, but chide myself for not being more dedicated even when I am doing the best I can. My best is never good enough and I am never satisfied. Will I always feel this way, or is this something peculiar to ballet dancing which I can gracefully drop when I stop dancing?

November 20th 1984

A pleasant day in Alex's company and I feel like living again, though my body is in painful knots from Uwe Scholz's complicated choreography.

I often wonder what it would be like not to have to do class every day: not to be in pain and exhausted from the work. The more I consider the idea of stopping dancing, the more attractive it appears. And yet, thinking about this helps me to enjoy the dancing more, just in the anticipation of the relief it would bring to stop. It is all very well to consider life without dancing, but I shall have to find something to replace it. Eventually I want to get my teaching diploma, teach and probably choreograph. But I have a strong urge to live as a "normal" person for a little while. The idea of returning to England and stopping dancing is very tempting. It would also bring me nearer to my father who misses me and suffers so dreadfully from his sciatica and spinal problems.

Yet I don't know how many choices I shall have as nothing has been mentioned to any of us on one-year contracts about next season. And then if I am offered another contract, will I be cast in any tempting parts? In a way I don't want to be tempted. This "talent" I have is such a bastard to live with. It is so demanding. It feels like a bad marriage. I wish I could divorce it sometimes. I recognise that the artistic flair inside me will always be there and one way or another I'll always have to live with it. But surely we shall be able to reach a compromise where I can keep it satisfied and still have a little freedom to eat ice cream with a free conscience, and not be forced to sweat my knotted muscles out of spasms? Would it make me a lesser person to give up this battle with my body? I constantly feel that I am fighting nature.

A year ago I remember telling Steve that I was afraid to return to England, but I was also afraid to stay in Sweden. Now I am afraid of feeling dead when I am alive; of the emptiness of being lonely, isolated and unable to find pleasure in anything.

November 25th 1984

I had a lovely surprise one evening when I found Alex waiting for me at the stage door after a performance. After watching the show he had waited for me to offer me a lift home. I didn't know that he was in the audience. That small gesture meant a lot to me.

Silent Song is becoming a duet for a male and a female, and I'm no longer dancing in it. Being able to observe other dancers in my movements has inspired a progression. The only problem is that the female dancer refuses to wear the *Ariadne* costume because she has danced in that ballet, and the association with the costume is too great. So I shall have to find her something else.

My colleague whose choreography I was dancing in has suddenly left the company. I don't know the reason, but I felt he was unhappy.

December 9th 1984

At last my period arrived; six miserable weeks late. This surely has contributed to my recent depression, despite attempts to distract myself with cinema, theatre, social engagements and long late night calls to Alex.

Nonetheless, my plans for a break from dancing are becoming more concrete. I have decided to return to London when my contract finishes in the summer and look for some non-dancing work. Perhaps I shall do a typing course, or whatever is necessary, to enable me to find employment. The biggest problem I foresee is breaking the news to my parents. They probably will not believe it is a rational decision. I'm so tired of the pain, the dieting, the loneliness, the disappointments, and the lack of rewards. Surely there is more to life than this? I am desperate for a break from it all.

December 29th 1984

Christmas at home was far from the joyous occasion we would have hoped. My parents are obviously disappointed by my decision. My mother has the most difficulty accepting it. How can I explain that something which was once a burning fire, an overwhelming need, has been burned out? I need the chance to prove to myself that I can live without Ballet; a period of abstention. Since I have been in Stockholm I have developed a habit of using work as a drug. I bury myself in an arabesque as if there is no tomorrow, not because I care about the arabesque, but because I am afraid of tomorrow. I escape into my work with a bitter intensity, and the more I do so, the more I question my motives.

My parents' basic opposition to my plans makes me feel even more isolated, but I seem to be finding strength within myself to cope, taking each day as it comes and enjoying the good parts. Just a ray of sunshine can make the world of difference to my mood.

I pace myself through my work, professionalism somehow keeps me going. I feel shattered. I long for a shoulder to cry on, someone to listen. Yet I don't want to burden my friends here and do not confide in them much. My diary is my best friend to which I can pour my heart out, causing it no pain or tedium. Often, I write myself into a better frame of mind.

My body is hurting so much again and I work through the pain as usual. Pain is becoming a habit and its addictive quality worries me a little. In order to cope with it and pull my technique together, concentration on my work makes me aloof. I am torn between trying to be friendly with my colleagues and trying to do my job properly. I am convinced I would be more relaxed about things if my private life were richer. Or is this just an excuse?

December 31st 1984

My longing for some physical comfort is causing Alex's company to verge on the frustrating. Just one hug would help so much. I ask myself what I'm doing here and why I don't just hop on the next plane back to London. All my belongings are organised. All I have to do is to pack the boxes and my suitcases. But I know I can't escape from myself, and I have to sort myself out. How do other people drag themselves out of the depths?

Little things are helping me to gradually feel in control: keeping my flat clean and organised, buying myself some new clothes and taking care of my appearance. Work has become a therapy. This year I'm staying home alone for New Year's Eve as tomorrow we have two performances of *Nutcracker*.

January 3rd 1985

The days roll by and slowly I feel calmer within myself. Herbal tranquillisers and an evening tipple of whisky help.

Silent Song is finished. It's about six minutes long. I'm not really satisfied with it; I seem to have reached a dead end. However, I have another idea for a short piece about waiting. Another sleepless night and I thought about the frustration of waiting: waiting to sleep, waiting for a performance, waiting for an opportunity, waiting to live, waiting to die … All our lives we are waiting.

A dancer will be seen in silhouette behind a screen. She is backstage preparing herself for a performance. The empty stage will be lit in front of the screen. After a while another dancer walks onto the stage as if the curtain is lowered and she is thinking about the role she will dance. She will go behind the screen and ask the other dancer what is happening.

The reply will be, "the audience is waiting".

Then she will ask, "what are they waiting for?"

Reply, "they are waiting for the ballet to begin".

"When will it begin then?"

"It has begun, it's about waiting".

"How boring!"

"Exactly!".

It is a silly idea but I have a very strong desire to present it, if only to alleviate my frustrations.

148

January 7th 1985

It continues to be very cold, around -12°C most of the time. The studios and my flat are well heated, so I'm surviving; so far. I've made friends with an English chap in the company. He has been here three years and it's interesting to hear that he has similar problems to me in coping with life in Sweden. Like me, he is considering returning to England and stopping dancing, though he is a talented dancer and still young. Only the Finns and Swedes seem to really feel at home here.

Alex is in my thoughts a lot. After another evening out and a cosy dance in a jazz club, I long for more than friendship, and I told him this. As our friendship has grown over the last two years, so has my affection. He certainly has a cuddly quality. Perhaps he has a girlfriend, or maybe he is not attracted to me anymore. Not only am I ready for more than work to fill my life, but I'm rather desperate for physical romance, especially as I feel let down since returning from Helsinki. I thought that success at the competition might help promote me here, but I feel I've regressed through having to prove myself all over again to the new director. I like working with Egon Madsen (the director) very much indeed, but he too is finding his feet in his new job. It's so hard to work with determined ambition when there seems to be nothing tangible to work for.

January 8th 1985
I feel I live on the edge of a cliff
Each moment so intensely
Full of excitement, danger, hope and fear
There is no tranquility
In the soul which longs to dive
Over the edge into adventurous seas.

January 14th 1985
Performances of *Taming of the Shrew* have started. I enjoy my part in the corps de ballet. In a week the second cast will dance Uwe Scholz's *Intermezzi*, and in two weeks there are the choreographic workshop performances which this year are open to the general public, rather than an invited audience like last year. Involvement is bringing back my inspiration. I am cast for a solo part in John Cranko's *Jeu de Cartes* in the spring premiere which tempts me to stay in Sweden just a little longer. However, I have not changed my plans and have started to teach myself to type. I'm constantly torn apart by indecision, and the black cloud of my father's poor health hangs over me.

149

January 18th 1985

Working with weights again, and doing specific exercises to strengthen the weaker areas around my hips and thighs, seem to be helping me to suffer less muscular pain and tune up my technique. I need to fine down as much as I can for the horribly revealing *Intermezzi* costumes. Now I have bronchitis instead. I just can't win! Jumping around and perspiring is doubtless not helping, but I have too much work to take any time off.

January 21st 1985

After my first performance of *Intermezzi*, battling with my nerves and rising to the challenge, I'm inspired to continue dancing. Everyone was complimentary about the second cast premiere and even Beryl Grey, who is here to cast her production of *Sleeping Beauty*, told me "mycket bra!" (very good) I found this hilariously funny until someone told me that she is married to a Swede and speaks Swedish. I suppose she doesn't know that I am English. Perhaps I was in a bad rut in the autumn, but my need to dance has not been drained as much as I thought. However, I still want to go home, so I'll investigate the possibilities yet again.

January 24th 1985

My emotions continue to yoyo; I'm sure the monthly blues have a lot to answer for. Alex and I are still friends, but he hasn't taken me up on my offer of more. I seem to have got over the intense frustration that was haunting me. Physical and emotional involvement in my work seem to have put animal instincts in their place, for the time being anyway.

I looked at the video of *Intermezzi*. None of us are shown to advantage in those white leotards and tights, but I can see how I need to stretch out the fronts of my thighs more and somehow straighten my pelvis. I look reasonably controlled and coordinated, but I want to take hold of myself like one of my sculptures and stretch out the area between the waist and knees. The battle with my body continues.

January 25th 1985

Suddenly life and work are fulfilling again. My parents - my mother in particular - are very relieved that I have changed my mind about giving up dancing, though I am still unsure about staying in Sweden.

The dress rehearsal for the choreographic workshop was another scary event. I showed *Birdsong* and this was the first time that Egon saw it, as well as the duet *Silent Song* and *Waiting*. My sense of humour in the last piece was shared by the audience and it was very satisfying to hear their laughter. It's marvellous to realise that I can communicate with an audience through my choreography. I received encouraging compliments from Egon and company members on all my pieces, even *Silent Song* which I had been unsure about.

January 26th 1985

The premiere was a big success and I'm enjoying performing *Birdsong* again too. Afterwards there was a meeting for the Ballet Club of the Opera House and the choreographers were interviewed. I hated speaking into the microphone and hearing my voice through the loud speakers. I surprised everyone though, including myself, by speaking in Swedish. Afterwards there was a party for the dancers and choreographers and I enjoyed the lively atmosphere and camaraderie. At last I have a real sense of belonging. I realise that although I miss my parents very much, my colleagues here are my family too. They are the ones who accept me as I am, who know my weaknesses and strengths. Dancers are held together by a respect for each other's struggles. We are a special breed. The bond between dancers is especially strong because of the emotional and physical trust between us. It's strange that this is the first time I seem to have realised this. I also realise that I am too deeply rooted in dance now to do much more than fantasise about abandoning it for very long.

We have started rehearsing *Jeu de Cartes*. It is a really fun piece to dance and thank goodness I wear a long skirt. There are more performances for the second cast of *Intermezzi*, and we continue to perform *Taming of the Shrew*, so life and work are pleasantly hectic.

It is -17°C!

January 28th 1985

I bumped into Egon in the corridor today who very diplomatically told me to take care of my weight, suggesting I could lose a little and pull up more in class. He said he'd noticed this in *Intermezzi*. Yes, so did I. I promised to try to fix it...

February 5th 1985

People are suddenly dropping like flies with sickness and injury and I lost both my dancers for *Silent Song*, one of whom was also in *Waiting*. Determined that the show would go on, I turned the former back into a solo with a variation on the choreography, found the costume from *Ariadne* which I had originally planned to use, and performed it myself. I also replaced the sick dancer in *Waiting*. I was terrified to speak on stage and to my shame made mistakes in my own script!

Fortunately, I had a second performance which went better and my spirit was boosted by complimentary reviews in the newspapers. *Dagens Nyheter* (02/02/1985) gave my pieces two paragraphs, with most praise for *Silent Song* as a solo, noting my "…calm intensity …" which was "…captivating." Even though I feel drastically overweight at 52 kilos, my fat does not inhibit the expression of my Art. This is so consoling.

February 10th 1985
During a week's holiday at home, I was much more optimistic than at Christmas, and peace has been made with my parents. Prospects of dancing in England are very bleak with no jobs available. Still undecided about the future, I intend spending my two months summer break at home to give myself a chance to experience how my life would be there. I also want to try to do a choreographic course at the University of Surrey. Friends tell me it's an excellent course for professional choreographers, dancers, composers and musicians.

Results of blood tests declare me to be fit and healthy. I mentioned my recent weight gain to my doctor who admitted that the medicine he had prescribed for my bronchitis might have caused this, though he didn't agree with me that this is a problem.

February 20th 1985
The cold weather continues and it is seldom above -10°C. But with frequent sunshine and clear blue skies, the snow sparkles brilliantly. I'm unable to break into a sweat when I dance and I never feel properly tuned up. They say it is possible to skate from Sweden to Finland, and the big ferries need ice breakers to make their path.

This evening I performed *Birdsong* at a charity gala to raise money for the famine victims in Ethiopia. It was a most satisfying way to contribute.

March 10th 1985
Life is enjoyable. Stage rehearsals for the next premiere are in progress and I love being the Ace of Spades in *Jeu de Cartes*. It calls for elegance and acting, no great technical feats. I am grouped with a King, a Knave and a Ten of Spades. We need a Queen to complete the set. The Two of Diamonds tries to join us, but we reject her in favour of the Joker who can, and does, push his way into all the sets of cards through the ballet.

I really feel underworked, but now my social life is expanding at last as I dedicate more effort to it, I'm able to enjoy my free time.

An evening out brought Alex and I close together on a disco floor and there was a mutual physical response. As we walked through the deserted streets later, we leant on each other in a playful, affectionate way. We arrived at his flat and I decided I would take a taxi home. Realising we would soon be parted I gave in to his advances which led to some passionate kisses. A taxi arrived to rescue me and I returned to my flat feeling somewhat mystified.

Alex and I see quite a lot of each other, but there has been no more suggestion of romance. Nonetheless, I am floating through the days on a high of being in love. I don't care if it's all in my head; I'm happy! My feelings were expressed in a poem I wrote on my return after that disco evening.

I stood on a cloud
Your hand reached for mine
And I followed.
I melted to your touch
Draped in submissive warmth
And I glowed.

March 17th 1985
There is still snow on the ground, but all I see is greenery. The sun is shining, the birds are chirping, I smell the scent of budding flowers and I see green leaves. Somewhere in the distance there is a long dark tunnel which I am so happy to have left behind. It is not magic, though it feels like it.

There was a buzz at the premiere last night and I felt as if I had wings on my feet. There are only four women in *Jeu de Cartes* and I was slightly sad that I was the only one not to receive flowers from friends or relatives. However, I remain high on my renewed discovery of joy in life. That is worth a thousand flowers.

March 25th 1985
A combination of my restless sense of urgency and the increasingly unpromising situation of the company here have spurred me to write to John Neumeier about the possibility of working in Hamburg. Egon continues to battle with the Opera director on behalf of the dancers and this is reflected in a general feeling of insecurity amongst us. Those of us on one year contracts still do not know if we will be offered work next season. I don't know if I could cope with living in Germany again, but I know I must do something positive about my future.

Alex has escaped to Austria for a skiing holiday. I miss him, but I have plenty of other friends and still spend a lot of time with Mia and her family.

March 31st 1985

The Opera from Tallinn in Estonia (which is part of the Soviet Union) has been guesting at the Opera House this week. Performances were sold out ages ago so I didn't attend any of them, but watched a little of the rehearsals from the wings. Yesterday an official buffet dinner was given by the city of Stockholm at the Town Hall for the Estonian visitors. Employees of the Opera House were also invited and I was one of the few dancers who chose to attend. I felt shy about going alone, but managed to summon the courage to do so. I found a place conveniently opposite the only man at my table. I broke the ice at my table by asking if anyone spoke English. The young man spoke some and soon we were involved in a stilted conversation. He told me that they receive Finnish television in Tallinn which shows English and American programmes. Tallinn is close to Finland with only a short stretch of sea between them. This was his first trip to Western Europe and it was very exciting for him. He works as a sound technician.

Later he offered to take me home. There was just sufficient time as he had to be back on the boat, in which the group from Estonia had travelled and slept, by midnight when his visa would run out. He told me that the police are very strict about checking passports. Tomorrow the boat sails back to Tallinn. It was a starry night and he gallantly offered me his arm as he escorted me back to my flat. He was very curious to see where I live and envied me having a flat to myself. He had to leave almost immediately and we agreed to write to each other so he could practise his English. I felt sad that I hadn't met him earlier in the week. I would have enjoyed showing him around Stockholm. It was also eerie to have made friends with a young man I am unlikely to meet again because of the political divide between East and West. I'm so glad that I have visited the Soviet Union because I can understand a little about his life.

April 11th 1985

How weird! How wonderful! Fate has finally given me an injury, timed to coincide with my mother's visit. At least she was able to see me onstage in *Nutcracker* and to witness my exotic backbend which has put me temporarily out of action. I've torn some muscle fibres in my back and I'm advised that the best cure is rest. Muscle relaxant tablets are easing the pain. Although I feel a little guilty about not being able to work, I also enjoy the excuse for a break.

I was apprehensive about my mother's visit after her dramatic outbursts at Christmas, but she seems happier now I've decided to continue dancing, though she still doesn't want me to go home. On the other hand, my father would love to have me home, whatever I decide to do with my life. Their conflicting attitudes only confuses my torn emotions more, and I still don't know if I shall be offered a contract for next year.

My mother relished the snow which is still thick here, and enjoyed a weekend away when we sailed through the giant ice blocks on the Baltic Sea to Åland, the island halfway between Sweden and Finland.

April 15th 1985
Waiting again …
Waiting for my back to heal; waiting for a reply to the letter I sent to Hamburg; waiting for news about the contracts here; waiting for information about the choreographic course this summer. I watched the postman through the peephole this morning and I just couldn't believe it when I saw him deliver letters through every door except mine. A little voice inside me said "you don't exist". I hate waiting!

April 20th 1985
Calling Hamburg gave me a positive feeling that I was doing something useful, but the unhelpful secretary would not put me through to John Neumeier. She told me that there is a pile of letters for him to go through, and it will probably take some time before I receive an answer. She also assured me that there are no vacancies.

April 23rd 1985
Apparently, I should be receiving a contract for next season with the Royal Swedish Ballet. I found out that everyone has received their contract except for me, and I was told that they are behind on their paperwork. This did not console me. My confidence is on a low ebb and I feel very out of touch with myself as I am not able to dance.

Some awaited post arrived at last - an application form for the choreographic course. Whatever happens next season I think it's important that I try to do this course.

April 30th 1985
I feel considerably more relaxed since my contract finally arrived, and was surprised and happy to notice that it includes a substantial pay rise.

155

The bonus actually brings my salary in line with that of a soloist which makes me feel more valued than I've felt for a long time. It also encourages me to stay in Stockholm next year and then perhaps audition for Hamburg.

I celebrated by buying myself the most expensive present yet: a colour television set. This is a way of making my life cosier and hopefully will help cheer the long dark evenings next winter. I'm still dreaming of being swept off my feet by a dashing viking, but I may as well accept that I am alone and make the best of it.

May 2nd 1985

I am 50% fit now and attended my first class today. Sweden is the only place I've been able to be half sick and half healthy. It means I can choose how much work I do and am under no obligation to do performances. It's a sensible arrangement allowing injured dancers to work themselves back into performing condition gradually. I've been doing floor exercises to maintain some strength in my muscles, but it was strange to be in class again. I felt curiously delicate, afraid to put stress on the healing back. I've only been away from class for three weeks; it must be dreadful for dancers who are off for months with more serious ailments. Being injured has been frustrating and I feel very fat and flabby. Now I'm full of good resolutions to get into shape again.

The cast lists for *Sleeping Beauty*, which is the first premiere next season, have gone up. My name appears for corps de ballet parts and Aurora's friends, but no solos. I'm disappointed about this, but there are other dancers with stronger classical techniques or better physiques than mine who are cast in the solo roles. People have suggested that my artistic quality and experience are worthy of a solo, but I don't want to complain and be reminded yet again of my imperfections. There will be a modern programme at the start of next season with ballets by Jiri Kylian, so I am really hoping I might be featured in this, but the cast lists are not on display yet.

May 10th 1985

My father arrived triumphant but exhausted on his motor bike having travelled by boat to Gothenberg, and then driven across country to Stockholm. Apparently, he was told by his doctor at home that he should go into hospital, but he decided to come and visit me instead. He is not well, but assures me he is making rapid progress with my nursing.

I continue to be confused with doubts about staying in Sweden. So I ask myself yet again, why am I here? I feel trapped: by ballet, by my life, by myself. I also feel terribly alone. I must be strong and resist the negative thoughts which are tempting me into a depressive abyss. It's probably all due to premenstrual tension anyway.

May 20th 1985

The Swedish spring really is magical; nature changes every day. Grass has sprung up inches from the bare soil in the last two weeks and buds are bursting into leaf on the trees. It's extraordinary how quickly things grow here.

I am thrilled to read on the cast lists that I am first cast for Jiri Kylian's *Ariadne* and second cast for his *Symfonietta*. At last I shall have the chance to dance his choreography. I am especially pleased about *Ariadne*. I loved it when I first saw it on a video, and then I used a costume from it for my own choreography. The other six dancers who did it two years ago are still here and keep their original places. So I am honoured to have been chosen for the only available place. This certainly gives me a sense of purpose for next season.

My father is much recovered and we've been able to make a few trips into the countryside on his motor bike discovering some beauty spots around Stockholm.

May 23rd 1985

I don't believe this, it is absurd! Just as I am reconciling myself to staying in Stockholm with a sense of purpose, a letter arrives from Hamburg inviting me to audition. Must I sacrifice Kylian for Neumeier, or vice-versa? Why must there always be a price?

I have started performing again after six weeks absence from the stage in the operetta *Orpheus in the Underworld*. This is a rare occasion when the ballet company is being used to perform in an opera production. Students from the ballet school are frequently used. It's an entertaining evening and dancing in the Cancan is amusing as the underworld costumes are punk style. Thus I wear multicoloured wigs and paint my face with a different design every performance, which is great fun.

May 28th 1985

The spring party was most enjoyable again this year, and as before the cabaret was the best part. A skit on *Birdsong* showed a chap gliding around on roller skates and flapping his arms in a pink skirt and plaited wig. It was hilarious. I like to be made fun of by my colleagues; it is a sign of respect. Most of the jokes are on the ballet staff and principal dancers. Again, I felt a sense of belonging and being a part of this company.

It is wonderful warm weather now and I feel restless and nervous with anticipation of the holidays and trip to Hamburg. I haven't breathed a word to any of my colleagues about going to Hamburg of course. I've decided to go there on my way to London. I'm not sure what I hope to achieve because there is no way I want to lose the chance of dancing in *Ariadne*. But somehow I feel I must go, and having a tangible goal helps motivate me through the last few weeks of season.

June 5th 1985

My cold has turned into a nasty cough and I have shin splints now as well. Determination keeps me fighting on. I went to see a doctor about my cough and am assured that it is not serious. My nervous tension is doubtless making everything worse. I was rather chuffed because the doctor, who is a ballet fan, recognised me from a workshop performance in January and told me how much he had enjoyed my dancing.

June 14th 1985

Preparations for Hamburg and the holiday continue as I pace myself through the days. I still don't know if my application for the choreographic course has been accepted, but I have permission to be free the first week of next season as the course overlaps with it.

Dieting is a constant struggle, but I've succeeded in fining down to an almost acceptable outline. I'm working with a vengeance but can't help feeling deflated when I still receive corrections on the placement of my pelvis in class. I know it's a fault I can only minimise rather than totally eradicate. It's demoralising to know that I'll never completely succeed, and accepting the struggle includes accepting a sense of failure.

June 23rd 1985

My fate was quickly decided. I cannot lie about the fact that I've signed a contract in Stockholm for next season, and this seems reason enough not to offer me a contract in Hamburg. However, I suspect that my uncertainty transmitted itself to John Neumeier causing him doubts about me. After three weeks preparing for this day I did not dance with confidence in my audition class. Perhaps destiny is warning me that I might not have the inner strength to cope with emotional survival here. Although it is a pleasant town, I haven't fallen in love with Hamburg as I did with Stockholm two and a half years ago, and I no longer have the steely ambition to achieve as a dancer which I would need in order to start again in a new company. It took guts to come here though, and it was a worthwhile thing to do.

Now I'm enjoying a few days holiday in Hamburg and observing the company in rehearsal and performance. The ballet mistress I stayed with before, when I came to perform *Birdsong*, has very kindly invited me to stay with her again. I also know a Swedish boy who came here from the Royal Swedish Ballet, so I almost feel part of the company for a short while. The buzz of creativity and commitment of the company is electric. John Neumeier has a wonderfully strong and supportive team around him, most of whom have been with him since he came to Hamburg. Some associations started as far back as the early days of his dancing career in Stuttgart. He has the support of the Hamburg State Opera House and the Hamburg public. He is a genius, but it seems to me that he is also a lucky genius.

The prospect of spending a third year in Sweden seems more promising when I realise that the situation and problems there are familiar, and therefore easier to deal with. Also, I can use my free time to develop my choreographic ideas. A strong feeling is growing inside me, even though I sometimes hate the isolation, that I must choreograph for myself. I am able to present the best of myself in a way which does not require a perfect balletic physique or technique. I should use my body as an instrument whilst I'm still able. There will be time enough to choreograph for other dancers in the future.

June 30th 1985
The overnight boat from Hamburg to Harwich brought me home to England and, my little adventure behind me, it's time to settle into a tranquil six weeks at home. It's good to know that I have been accepted on the choreographic course, though not as a choreographer as I had hoped, but as a dancer. I'm sure I'll learn a lot and be stimulated by meeting new, like-minded people, and the creative environment.

July 4th 1985
I'm trying to relax after the recent build up of tension, but it's shocking how quickly I have blown up into feminine curves which just should not belong to a ballet dancer's figure. I feel nature fighting inside my body as though it wants me to be feminine; a reproductive instrument. Rather than feeling like a bulbous pig, I feel like a very frustrated female. My skin tingles and longs to be touched and my mind wanders helplessly into fantasies of warm, comforting arms, strong thighs, sex and even babies. I feel emotionally like a teenager who dreams of romantic love. I am

159

old enough and experienced enough to know that reality is another story, but even so, I do feel dreadfully frustrated by the unnatural pattern of my life. It's easier to accept when I'm busily involved with my dancing. It's hard now because I'm allowing myself to relax and forget about dancing for a bit. I know that I need this break very much, but I have to come out of it respecting myself as a dancer. So I must try to take care of my weight.

July 13th 1985

I'm sitting up late watching the "Live Aid" concert raising money for Ethiopian famine relief. It is special to be aware that I'm sharing this programme with viewers all over the world; a union of human souls in the name of a good cause. I have put a note with the cheque I am sending which sums up how I feel. It says, "Thank you for your Live Aid concert and bringing some unity of spirit to this unbalanced world we live in with your quest to help save Ethiopia".

The images of the starving people are distressing and moving, and I feel ashamed to place such importance on my relatively trivial problems and frustrations. I wish I could care more about other people and less about myself; be more of a human being and less of an egocentric drip! But I'm not sure how I'll manage this until I stop dancing, as it takes discipline and single-mindedness twenty-four hours a day to keep my body in check.

July 24th 1985

Mostly I like having the house to myself whilst my parents are in Switzerland on holiday. Only in the evenings I am sometimes frightened that there might be an intruder. The crime rate is considerably higher in London than in Stockholm and this worries me a little. However, the opportunity to be alone in London is convincing me that this is my home and I need to return here. It just feels so right to be here. There is no need to be lonely when I have so many friends around, and I can turn on the television or radio anytime and understand it perfectly. I miss this so much in Sweden.

August 2nd 1985

Images are forming in my mind of returning to London after a third season in Stockholm and doing the teaching course. Signing another contract, if I were offered one, would involve a long term commitment; a permanent position with a pension waiting for me at the end of it. It is not possible to have a one-year contract for more than three years. What would I do with the rest of my life in Sweden?

****

August 26th 1985

I have returned to Stockholm inspired after the two-week Gulbenkian International Choreographic Summer School for professional choreographers and composers at Surrey University.

As I had hoped, it proved tremendously stimulating. Everyone came for slightly different reasons with varying goals in mind. We all shared a sense of excitement at the opportunity to be challenged in an informal environment in our respective fields as choreographers, dancers, composers and musicians. It was a big party of the best sort, playing with creative ideas and responding to different tasks. There was a friendly and informal atmosphere with everyone being an equally essential part of the whole. I made friends with a Polish choreographer with whom I spoke French, and a Dutch composer. People had come from all corners of the globe to participate, and I appreciated the chance to work with all of the choreographers at least once. The course was tough physically and I had the predictable difficulties coping with this. However, I managed not to get seriously injured which, unfortunately, some did not.

A typical day started with an hour and a half ballet class with Ivan Kramar (from the Dutch National Ballet) at 9am, then a short break followed by an hour and a half contemporary class with the course dance director Robert Cohan (from London Contemporary Dance Theatre). It was good to revisit Martha Graham contemporary technique and this will also help me with *Ariadne*. Then there was a lecture, or discussion about the day's project before lunch. After an hour's lunch break there were four hours of work on the project in small groups, followed by an hour for dinner before the creations were presented, videoed and discussed. It was unusual to finish before 11pm.

There was very little time for the choreographers and composers to discuss their ideas and they worked under tremendous pressure. I was glad not to be choreographing, but able to learn from my involvement as a dancer and by observation. I appreciated learning from other people's mistakes without having to make my own for all to see. Everyone was charmingly sincere and open about discussing imperfections and ways of improvement. It was tough for the choreographers and composers to be given a new task each day. Sometimes the ideas flowed, sometimes they didn't. The challenge for the dancers was to grasp as much as possible from a choreographer's spirit in just a few hours, to help him or her to show the new work as well and as clearly as possible. Sometimes we didn't hear the music till the actual presentation. Food and drink were plentiful and we were encouraged to take a daily cocktail of vitamin pills. Alcoholic cocktails were available until 1am when the bar closed. At the end of the first week I was relieved to be in a piece where all I had to do was take five minutes to peel an apple. What a welcome break from the rushing around in the previous choreographies!

The second week I had a minor foot injury which restricted what I could do, but somehow the choreographers managed to use me, even if it was rolling on the floor. There was a massive party the last evening which continued until dawn as everyone let rip after the extraordinarily intense fortnight.

September 1st 1985
I had been thinking about Alex a lot and missing him over the summer, so it was a lovely surprise when he turned up at my door soon after I arrived back. He said he was just passing by and didn't stay long, but I was really glad to see him.

I've plunged straight into performances of *Orpheus in the Underworld* and amaze myself by my professionalism. I look forward to doing *Ariadne* and am full of ideas for new choreography which I try out in the theatre studios when they are free. One of my projects is to rework *Silent Song* as a longer solo for myself.

Nonetheless, life feels very intense again since I am back in Sweden. It's a constant struggle to keep on top of my emotions; they were so much more subdued in England. Here they seem to have a razor sharp edge. I'm determined to go home next year and to do the professional dancer's teaching course at the Royal Academy of Dance in London, and am applying to authorities both here and in England for a grant. In the meantime, I am trying to cultivate my social life to avoid too much isolation.

September 15th 1985
Following a long silence Alex called me and we went to see a film together. He confided his love life to me for the first time, and I feel less rejected now I know there has been another woman in his heart recently. I have not confided to him how much I fantasise about him. Perhaps it's better to stay friends.

Work revolves around preparing for the premiere of *Ariadne* and I'm happy to have this to work towards. I'm learning *Sinfonietta* but disappointed that the second cast is not scheduled to perform it.

I met Gunilla Roempke (my former director here) in the Opera House canteen. She was on the jury at the International Ballet Competition in Moscow this summer, and she told me that people asked after me and are still talking about my *Birdsong*. This news gave me great joy of course and helped me to find the courage to give a talk on the making of the solo to the Ballet Club connected to the Opera House. I told stories of my experiences creating the piece as I demonstrated parts of it. People warmed to me immediately, laughing spontaneously and applauding when I related my visit to the zoo in Copenhagen where I accused an exotic bird of stealing my choreography. At the end I performed the entire solo. It was enormously satisfying to have such a close contact with the audience.

September 25th 1985

This week is dominated by rehearsals of *Ariadne*. I am overcoming the physical problems for the floor work and deep back bends, but not without pain and bad bruises. The rolling around on the floor is particularly challenging on the steep rake of the Opera house stage. The theme is based on the Greek myth of Ariadne, wife of Dionysos, the God of wine and ecstasy. In this depiction she sacrifices herself to a new life of ecstasy through the excessive use of drugs in secret rituals. Each of the seven female dancers reflects a facet of Ariadne, and at the end of the thirty-minute piece the dancers feel as if they too have passed into another world.

We have a new company member who is replacing a sick dancer. She and I are quickly becoming friends, bonding over similar concerns of coping with pain and deciding what path our futures should take. At last I can confide in someone who understands how I feel. The same age as me, she too appreciates our sharing of thoughts and dilemmas.

September 27th 1985

As I lay awake last night trying to avoid lying on my painfully swollen bruises and irritated by a sore throat, I asked myself the old question, "what on earth am I doing to myself?" I remembered how purposeless life had seemed almost a year ago, and of the black hole I almost fell into. I could have killed myself for nothing then. Now I have *Ariadne*, and I must be prepared to die for it if I am to see my way through the pain, as I roll on my bruises onstage tomorrow night.

When I fell asleep I had a weird dream about escaping from a sinking ship by diving into the sea, even though I can't swim. I was rescued by the comfort of a man's body wrapped around mine guiding me to the safety of the shore. The sensation of our nude bodies clinging together in the water was soothing. When I woke this morning I felt able to face the challenge of the premiere. My efforts later were rewarded by receiving flowers from both the direction and my parents. The former bouquet included a powder dose of aspirin in a sachet, not for the flowers but for me; initiation into the pained, drugged world of *Ariadne*.

October 17th 1985

After the first few performances of *Ariadne* there was a break from it during which my body appreciated the opportunity to heal. We show it again at the end of the month.

I've started exploring the contemporary dance scene in Stockholm and am generally disappointed. Choreographers can be so self-indulgent; endless repetition of meaningless movements. I don't understand it at all. I was introduced to some students from the three-year choreographic course at the Danshögskolan (High School of Dance). It is stimulating to exchange ideas with them as I try to develop myself as a creator of movement and dance. The hours I spend alone in the studio trying out new ideas are invaluable, and I seem to instinctively set myself tasks similar to those of the Swedish course.

The students were interested to hear about how I talk aloud to myself, vocalising my movements in preparation for communicating my ideas to the dancers. Otherwise, after spending hours planning movements alone, it can be quite daunting to find oneself unable to express one's intentions in words to the dancers. I have to feel at one with my thoughts and movements before I ask the performers to interpret them. I must know what I want and how to talk about it. I think that the pace of a rehearsal is lost if there are long periods of silence whilst the choreographer thinks through ideas. I prefer to do the thinking part in privacy as much as possible. It even takes practice to be uninhibited in solitude in the ballet studio. I noticed how difficult it was working with choreographers who didn't know what they wanted, or didn't believe in their ideas, during the course in the summer. I want to inspire my dancers' confidence by being positive myself about my goals.

It makes such a difference to life to have a close girlfriend at work. Another new friend is a male dancer in the company who is also a keen choreographer. All three of us often sit together in the canteen chatting away. These two are soul mates, but I also have a little circle of other friends in the company now too. I go out with my dancer friends much more regularly and spontaneously than during the last two years when my focus was on saving my energy and dieting. I still spend time with my English neighbour, Mia and her family, and Alex and his friends. The

164

moments alone become fewer and further between, and the loneliness is less frequent.

October 23rd 1985
Developing *Silent Song* is a demanding challenge and it grows slowly as I experiment with the full circle skirt which will be the new costume. I am incorporating it into the movement, using it to dramatic effect. Friends I trust are my "eyes" watching the choreography as it progresses and giving me feedback. Sometimes I receive opposition to creating in silence, so it was encouraging to hear a composer announce that he likes pure Art forms, such as dance in silence. I believe that so long as one uses the silence consciously, it is perfectly valid.

Rehearsals for *Sleeping Beauty* with Beryl Grey are enjoyable. She is a remarkable woman, bursting with energy, and I do enjoy having an English influence at the theatre. I like dancing in this production and enjoy it for its own sake, without a cloud of ambition hanging over me. My greatest pleasure is in the way the entire company is brought together like a big family. This feeling of togetherness is often lost with dancers being split into different dressing rooms, and rehearsals.

November 1st 1985
This evening I feel like an addict who is denied his drug and suffers withdrawal symptoms. The final performance of *Ariadne* was cancelled at a few hours' notice because of a dancer's injury. So I went to the theatre even though I was free, and worked on my choreography. I've been working on a solo to music by Brahms for a while. It's almost finished, but I don't like it much. It's has no originality, though I've enjoyed playing with movements and ideas. Now I have a new project, a piece about London putting my perpetual homesickness to productive use. All I know is that it starts with Big Ben striking twelve. The rest is an unknown adventure which I shall discover as I go along. I made myself spend time in the studio thinking about the new piece, but inspiration did not flow and I made little progress. I try to push myself when I work alone with the thought that, maybe one day, I'll have enough material to create a one woman show.

November 4th 1985
It is peculiar, rather luxurious, to be in love (I use the words lightly) with someone I work with. No tense moment, will he ask me out again? Just a simple, see you tomorrow. No commitments, no unnecessary tangle of emotions. One of my colleague's attentions towards me used to verge

on an irritation, and all of a sudden I'm finding them curiously attractive. Now we go out together to eat or see a performance quite often, and our friendship is very warm. I'm a little wary of the situation, perhaps he is too, as we both plan on leaving the company. However, work at the Opera House takes on a whole new dimension with a little flirtation, counter balanced by the stability of a close girlfriend.

Life is a wonder. What an intricate tapestry of emotional texture we create through our little daily experiences. I am happy I have the ability to recognise and enjoy so many treasures of being alive, and the gift to express myself as an artistic student of life. I feel as if my life is like the contents of a novel as I turn over a new page with curiosity to discover the next adventure which awaits me.

November 6th 1985

At a dress rehearsal of *Sleeping Beauty* today I slipped into the auditorium when I was not needed onstage and watched from different places. I felt as if I was on some kind of outing and had to laugh at myself to think that I was being paid for it. I was struck by the intimacy of the Opera House, even from the highest balcony. It was strange to realise that the stage is the nucleus of the theatre. It is so obvious, but easy to forget when one is totally absorbed by the challenges of performance. I wandered around in my layers of dance wear and stage makeup cheerfully greeting the cleaners. We were each involved with our daily work, but our duties are a hundred miles apart. All the energy and activity which are in progress every day in all corners of the Opera House ultimately serve the stage and the performance. The world I live in as a performer is the little ball of fire at the core of it all, receiving all the energy in order to give it out again to the audience. I can see a likeness to the core of a woman which is served by the mechanism of the outer parts to ultimately bring forth the creation of new life. *Sleeping Beauty* looks lavish and tasteful, and I feel proud to be a part of this beautiful classic production in such a perfect theatrical setting.

Later I took a studio and to my surprise movement poured from my body. I felt as if there were devils inside me banging on my muscles screaming to be released. Some escaped but there are thousands more tearing at me within.

November 20th 1985

The joy of *Sleeping Beauty* is that it doesn't drain me and I have energy left over to work at my choreography and to socialise. Consequently, I see a lot of both my theatre friends and my "normal" friends. It's so wonderful to feel surrounded by them.

Some colleagues and I made an excursion to Gothenberg in a hire car and three of us took turns driving the five-hour route. We saw a performance and met up with dancers from the company there. One of the dancers had been in Düsseldorf with me and it was strange to meet again. The countryside was pretty in the snow and we all enjoyed the opportunity of a change. I wrote a little poem after driving on the icy roads in the dark, which required some courage and faith as I haven't driven a car for a long time. Although the poem is about driving, it is also about living.

I was afraid of driving in the dark
Until I discovered
That the road unravelled itself before me
As long as I trusted it would
And kept driving.

November 28th 1985
I've started teaching the London inspired solo to a colleague. I am straying from my original idea and it's turning into something else, though I don't know what yet; probably a piece for several dancers. I can already see the end with the dancers moving in unison for the first time as one spirit, but I have a long journey before I reach it. It is very satisfying and I'm much calmer when working with others. I can get pretty neurotic working alone. I feel more comfortable when I can be detached and stand on the production side. I feel I am preparing myself for life as a choreographer and teacher, and looking at things from an objective, intellectual angle, rather than from a purely subjective, emotional point of view.

November 30th 1985
I received a letter from the Opera House today informing me that my contract will not be renewed. As I wasn't seriously planning on staying I can't be too upset. I would surely have been tempted if I had been offered a permanent contract now I am feeling more at home here. Nonetheless, I feel as if a black cloud as lifted off me. It feels more like a release from a prison sentence, or army service, than a rejection. Other contracts have not been renewed either, so I am not alone.

Considering whether to stay in Sweden and take my chances as a freelance dancer and choreographer, or return to England, I had a long discussion with Egon. He was warm and offered to help me in any way he can, but he warned me that long term prospects for me here are not promising. He is convinced I would be better able to develop my choreography in England. Whenever an opportunity arises here, a Swede will inevitably be put before me. It is clear that Egon and his wife have not been able to settle into life here and they too will soon be leaving.

Doubts are arising in my mind about the wisdom of doing a teaching course when I want to choreograph. But I need to make a living, and being able to teach and choreograph will open more doors for me. I am getting to know some of the staff at the Royal Swedish Ballet School and observe classes and performances there with great interest. Christopher Bruce, one of my favourite choreographers, is working with the company. I am not involved in his piece but relish the opportunity to sit in on his rehearsals and watch him work. So, when I am not busy doing my paid job of dancing, I am researching in preparation for the new path I shall take.

December 3rd 1985

There are frequent problems with the lift at the Opera House. The stage is on level four and the ballet dressing rooms are on level eight, so dancers often use them. This evening a lift got stuck between floors trapping four dancers (including me) and two singers. We were there for twenty minutes before we were rescued. The dancers were hoping to miss an entrance. However, we heard our music just as we were helped out of the lift. We dashed onto the stage to find the others jumping around madly improvising to try to compensate for our absence. It was impossible to take the performance seriously after this. It's lucky it happened during *Orpheus in the Underworld* and not *Sleeping Beauty*.

December 6th 1985

We have started rehearsing Bronislava Nijinska's *Les Noces*. I don't expect to perform it but it's an interesting experience to learn this classic piece from Les Ballets Russes, and I really enjoy Igor Stravinsky's richly textured music for percussion, pianists, chorus and solo singers. I am a cover for the next triple bill premiere and my heart really isn't in it.

December 15th 1985

News from home is that my father's back has been very bad recently and the pain is causing him severe depression. I ask myself how long this can go on, and how it will end. I'm glad I'll see him at Christmas. I just hate being so far away, but who knows if my proximity will really help when I return in the summer. At least I shall no longer have to live with a sensation of being wrenched apart all the time.

Mozart's *Requiem* is my therapy. It's so soothing, I listen to it often, sometimes several times a day. It's like a calm companion. I particularly love the "Lacrymosa" section.

December 20th 1985

Now I have decided to do the teaching course and move into the production rather performing side of my profession, I find it hard to continue to be a dancer. Dancing demands 200% commitment from me and I barely have 50% left to give. Somehow I'm going to have to survive the next six months of my contract. I have to be practical about my work and less emotional. Surely it is not in any way bad to do my job as employment and avoid sentimentality? As far as my life away from work is concerned, there is no way I would survive without my friends, but it is hard not to hope for more.

What I don't understand, is that I get the distinctive feeling that men find me attractive. I ask myself what it is that they see in me which I don't see in myself? What is it about me that makes me mysteriously attractive but untouchable to these men?

A peculiarly disturbing experience today was when a middle-aged dresser at the theatre plucked up the courage to tell me that he is in love with me. He said he goes weak at the knees when he sees me, and thinks I am the most beautiful woman. Would he believe that I am as lonely as him? All I can do is smile and be polite.

December 28th 1985

Seeing my parents at Christmas brought me face to face with the realities of their problems; my father's bad health, and coping with it. It is a tremendous stress for my mother too. A cloud hangs over me whether I am here or there. But proximity gives me the chance to deal with the emotional response to a reality, rather than an abstract anxiety. There is also hope that I can help in some way when I am there, which is impossible when I am here. I was rather shocked to see books on display about what to do when someone dies. They argue so much, why can't they try to work on quality of life whilst they still have it? I wanted to make a joke about the books on the lines of, "when are you thinking of knocking me off then?" But I didn't manage it. It might have been prudent to put the books out of sight whilst I was home over Christmas. Or did they want me to see them, as if they think I don't know how serious the situation is? On the other hand, I still get vibes from my mother that I should not return to England and will not be welcome at home when I do.

January 1st 1986

New Year's Eve 1985 was one of my best, a happy contrast to 1984. After two performances of *Nutcracker*, I went to a party with theatre friends not leaving till 7am this morning in order to catch a little sleep before the performance of *Orpheus in the Underworld* this afternoon. Apart from my travel card being out of date (it didn't occur to me that I wouldn't have a chance to buy one for January), and the bus driver growling at me as he made me pay for a ticket, it seemed a good start to the year.

January 4th 1986

I am a little in love with two different male friends: Alex, and a friend in the company. Either of them could seduce me so easily, and yet they do not. Perhaps they are too busy searching for themselves, whereas I am searching, or hoping, for a partner with whom to grow through the experience of a loving relationship.

January 10th 1986

I've decided to give up being in love, for the present anyway, as life revolves around the work schedule again. It's chaotic with people falling sick all the time and I find myself shuffled around in different places in *Sleeping Beauty*. I like this as it keeps my brain fresh and saves the performance from becoming monotonous. There is the promise of another choreographic workshop, but a date hasn't been set. At least it gives me hope and a goal to work towards.

January 24th 1986

I've amazed myself by my pushiness in persuading my friend in the company, who also choreographs, that he needs me as ballet mistress and stage manager for his trip to the choreographic competition in Paris next month. As he is dancing in his own piece with two other dancers, he needs someone he trusts to be his "eyes" for him. He will also need someone who speaks French to cue the lights and sound at the performance. I qualify for both these jobs. He has a grant covering travel and accommodation for four people and is renting an apartment for a week. As I am not involved in performances that week, I've been able to persuade Egon that I may have permission to go.

February 3rd 1986

This is a beautiful day in my life. I woke to find myself lying in Alex's arms this morning. Yesterday evening after an outing to the cinema and dinner, neither of us wanted to part. When the kissing started, I was determined not to make the same mistake as last year, and I allowed myself to melt. It was so special to make love with Alex after wanting to for so long. A similar height to me, our bodies wrap around each other with natural comfort. It seemed to me that he felt the same way and neither of us slept much as we cuddled through the night. He was sensitive to my feelings and needs, accepting that I am "out of practice", although I don't think he believes it is almost four years since I slept with a man. It's just so good to feel like a human being again. I often asked myself if it would feel different to go to class in the morning after having slept in a lover's arms. Now I discover that it doesn't feel different, it feels right. To wake up alone simply feels wrong. I'm calm and confident about our relationship. We have known each other two years and this seems a natural extension of our friendship.

February 7th 1986

This is an extraordinary week for me. I am constantly high on happiness. The prospect of Paris and the preparation for it as I help with rehearsals, is just as thrilling as the development in the relationship with Alex. In addition to all this I'm working on my choreography.

The piece for three dancers is a struggle, deciding what I want, and also simply coordinating everyone's schedules, when we are all available and there is a free studio. Solving the problems of making a dance piece with no plot or musical form, and irregular attendance by my dancers, means that I have to create it all from scratch. Little by little, images are forming in my mind and I envisage the shape of things to come. Anyway, I'm blissfully happy to be involved in so many nice things.

February 10th 1986

So I am back to my "stable" relationship with myself it seems … How ironic: Alex can't have a physical relationship with me without feeling a dutiful sense of commitment, and I can only consider such a relationship with a close friend, or at least someone I know and care about. He tells me that I am his "best friend" and "it means something if you sleep with your best friend." I suppose he is avoiding the responsibility of developing our relationship. Perhaps he is right to put a stop to it now. I have my doubts about our compatibility for a long-term future, but that wouldn't stop me from enjoying the moment. Still I don't regret last week because it helped me to regain some confidence in my femininity.

February 17th 1986

I am back in Stockholm feeling somewhat disorientated and rather exhausted after a week in Paris.

First impressions were of a metropolis which is even dirtier than London. I was surprised by the number of tramps sleeping in the metro, the absence of rubbish bins and therefore littered streets, the polluted air, the inefficiency and lack of organisation. There were no train timetables and one evening we unwittingly missed the last train and ended up walking several kilometres to the flat. The competition was very badly organised and the only reliable thing about it was that it always ran late!

It was like spring in Paris compared to frozen Sweden and at least 10C warmer. This was certainly welcome and it was such a pleasure to see fresh flowers on sale. The flat we stayed in was small, cosy and typically Parisian with a wonderful iron railing on the balcony. I assumed the role of "mother", doing all the cooking and taking care of everyone, even massaging the dancers' sore bodies. I think this was as necessary for them as my assistance as ballet mistress. Throughout the week there was a family atmosphere between the four of us which was incredibly satisfying. It was a welcome distraction from the painful sense of rejection I was living with.

There was a reception at the lavish town hall where, to my surprise, I met an Italian choreographer who had been at the choreographic course last summer. He was also entering a piece in the competition. We watched some of the preliminary rounds as well as the finals. All the finalists were in an experimental vein, contrary to the more classically based piece which we had brought, and most of them were French.

Although our days revolved around the competition, there was time for sightseeing. Mostly I enjoyed wandering around the streets, especially along the river Seine and in the Latin Quarter. We also visited landmarks such the Louvre and the Pompidou centre, and had some nice meals out in the quaint restaurants of Montmartre near the flat.

February 25th 1986

It is "sportlov", an official Swedish holiday so everyone can go away skiing. This year the company has its break at the same time as the schools which is convenient for the parents in the company, but makes travel more expensive. So I decided to stay in Stockholm and work rather than going home where the atmosphere is very tense. There are voluntary classes every morning in which I participate, and afterwards I work on my choreography. I have found a choreographic soul mate in a woman who teaches modern dance and danced for many years with the Culberg

Dance Company. She is just beginning to explore a choreographic outlet and we are both at the same point of having ideas and needing a sympathetic body and soul to work them out on. We have been having "jam sessions", as my choreographer friend I went to Paris with calls them, where we try out our movements on each other and discuss our ideas. It is wonderfully stimulating. We share a foundation of classical ballet and Martha Graham techniques which seems to help us tune in to each other.

March 10th 1986
The big thaw has started and there is promise of spring in the air. My life revolves around work with a lot of performances. A couple of good friends at work have left the company and I really miss them.

At last a date has been set for the choreographic workshop and it will be at the end of this season. This gives me a reason to stay here as there is not much else apart from collecting my salary.

March 12th 1986
Today was an inspiring one as I had time to work on my choreography. A third dancer has joined the cast of *Untitled* as the piece which was originally about London is now called. I'm exploring new territory in this; making it a slow, somewhat tedious process. However, the new member of the team is a good choice with her enthusiasm, creativity and elasticity in her movements which is exactly what I want.

Later, I started work on a short duet from Benjamin Britten's Serenade for tenor, horn and strings. It is to a poem by William Blake, "O rose thou art sick". I'm making it for two volunteers who want more work. It's so easy to work with music again, the ideas fall into place so much quicker than working in silence or with sound effects as in *Untitled*.

March 14th 1986
Surprise…surprise… a phone call from Alex. "Where have you been hiding?" he asked me. Hiding? He seemed keen to see me, but I postponed a meeting. I'm tired and sore, and pain killers are getting me through my work. It's delicious to think that soon I shall no longer have the pressure of performance, but as long as I do, my professional pride still pushes me to do the best I can.

March 15th 1986
Stockholm is in mourning today for the funeral of Olof Palme the Swedish prime minister. It is a horrid grey day, in fact we haven't seen the sun since he was shot two weeks ago. The implications of this assas-

sination have upset the Swedish population enormously. They were so sheltered in their peacefulness. It was eerie last week when there was an official minute of silence at midday. I was outside at the time and people stopped still in the street. A few obviously had not heard what was happening, or perhaps they were tourists, and they received sideways glances of distaste from the stationary pedestrians.

Later I watched the reports on television about the funeral. Everyone was wiping their faces with hankies; the mass mourning was quite moving. Some people looked as if they didn't understand what they were grieving for. They seemed to go along to put a rose on the grave looking miserable because everyone else did.

March 20th 1986

It's becoming a habit to unplug my telephone and I'm very unsociable. There are a lot of performances which are an ordeal and drain me totally. It's not easy to pretend to be lively onstage and put on a smiling face when I am tired, my body hurts and I know that soon I shall not perform any more. I don't have any time or energy for my choreography when the schedule is so full and I really miss it.

Waiting again … waiting for it to be over. It is difficult for me to communicate, even with friends, and it must be hard for them to understand me. Alex phoned again, but I cut the call short. I feel so wretched, I can't give out any energy at all. I feel I'm pushing my friends away just at a time when I could use their support. The therapy of confiding in the pages of my diary helps so much.

March 23rd 1986

It's snowing! Winter isn't over yet.

That's the bad news. The good news is that I slept thirteen hours last night and have awoken feeling much refreshed. I suspect the dream I had about kissing and cuddling a tall, handsome man has a lot to do with my improved spirits. I wish I could have a stable relationship to give me the chance to find out whether all those kisses and cuddles are as important as I think they are. I was surprised how quickly I forgot what it was like to be alone and frustrated, during that short week with Alex. It's like two different planets; to be alone, or to have a man in my life. And when I'm on one, I can't imagine what it's like to be on the other. I wonder if I had the sort of regular loving attention I long for I'd feel a permanent change, or if after a while I'd take it all for granted and feel ratty again.

March 27th 1986

The fight to keep going continued. The days seemed so long, sometimes it was as much as I could do not to break down in tears onstage, let alone dance with inspiration. Now however, the last performance is over for a few weeks and we are not scheduled to have such an intense performing period again this season.

One evening an older dancer asked me if I would stand for her as a courtier in Act Three of *Sleeping Beauty*. I am very fortunate as I usually sit as a court lady watching the dances, but all the men and a few women have to stand. She was obviously feeling dreadful otherwise she would never have asked, so we exchanged places. It made me sad to think that it is the fate of so many of the older corps de ballet members to decorate the stage whilst they watch the younger ones dancing the solos. Surely these people have more to offer after some twenty years professional experience, and the direction could cultivate these resources?

April 1st 1986

A few days break over Easter was most welcome. After the recent pressure it felt like school holidays!

My neighbour recorded a programme about the Opera House on television and I saw myself on the screen looking horrendous in thick layers of dance clothes, trying to hide from the camera in our pre-performance warm up. It was curiously depressing to watch this programme as I thought of the abandoned hope for what might have been. The Royal Swedish Ballet has so much to offer with the rich repertoire, the beautiful theatre and luxurious facilities. It is ideal for some people, those perhaps who feel at home in Sweden and have their roots here, but not for me. I appreciate the opportunity and have gained enormously during my three years here from such a rich experience. But I can't make myself into something contrary to my nature and upbringing in order to fit into this way of life and working, for the sake of a few superficial attractions.

I've arranged for a video to be made in a few days of *O rose thou art sick* as the dancers I'm working with will be leaving Stockholm next week. So this evening I was determined to finish it, which, in a great burst of energy, I did. I have never worked so fast. The four-minute piece has been completed in three rehearsals. This is an excellent experience for me because usually I seem to choreograph slowly, analysing each stage. It might be useful to develop some speed and it was exciting to see the entire piece materialise so quickly before my eyes.

Sometimes I have imagined what my desires would be if I discovered that I only had a limited time left to live. I used to fantasise about how I would eat chocolate, cakes and all my favourite foods before my time ran out. Now, having abandoned the eternal sacrifices of dieting and paid the price of extra flab, my desire would be to finish my choreography and to see my parents. My mental focus has changed and I wonder how much time I have wasted counting calories, bingeing and starving.

April 4th 1986

What a disappointment, but this is typical of my profession. One of my dancers has injured himself and *O rose tho art sick* could not be videoed. I shall just have my notes as a record. It would have meant so much to have it on video.

We are rehearsing Kenneth MacMillan's *Romeo and Juliet*. I might have hoped for a character role in it if I were not leaving. I should have loved to do the dramatic part of Lady Capulet, Juliet's mother. I am cast in the corps de ballet and thankfully I don't have to cover anything. I love the production but rehearsals are tedious. I am looking forward to a week's break in London when I shall audition for the teaching course at the Royal Academy of Dance.

BBC World Service is keeping me company. What an unusual joy that it is so clear. I get very annoyed when the reception is bad or impossible, and I am desperate to hear an English voice. I pace around my little flat rattling the radio, turning the aerial in all directions frantically searching for a clearer sound. The other disappointment is when I switch it on hopefully and there is a football match!

I've joined a film club which shows many foreign films, and even dance films, through the day and evening in several cinemas in Stockholm. This might help me pass the time as I wait to leave Stockholm.

A Hungarian film made a big impression on me. It was poetic throughout and I particularly liked the end when the hero struggled to swim across the river Danube determined to make it to the other side as his father had done before him. We saw him in close-up battling with the currents, then the picture widened to show a head appearing behind his shoulder. The ghost of his father perhaps? Then there were dozens of swimmers behind him. Were they chasing him? Or was it the director's way of saying that we may all feel isolated in our personal endeavours in life, but actually everyone is struggling in the same sea of life in their own way? It confirmed to me the validity of the conclusion of my piece *Untitled* where, one by one, the dancers come to move in harmony in an endless circle.

April 12th 1986

My audition for the teaching course in London last week was successful and I've been officially accepted. I wish I didn't have to wait till September to start, but I still have to try to get some funding to pay for the course.

Although it was lovely to be home, my parents both commented on how much weight I have gained. To them, my fat represents a lack of discipline. They have no appreciation for the very deep inner strength which keeps me alive. To me, my fat represents the conflicts and confusions in my emotions. I have considered suicide as an option since I have lived in Sweden, mostly because I suffer such guilt and shame over no longer being skinny. My decision to give up dancing last winter was an alternative to ending my life. Do they think I have no value if I am not a skinny dancer? My mother is appalled that they allow me to dance onstage in a tutu here. She obviously thinks my fat is worse than the company direction think it is. I know that getting thin will not solve anything for me, but learning to accept and believe in myself will help tremendously.

I consider the condition of anorexia nervosa, where there are psychological reasons a girl becomes a childlike skeleton, sometimes in a subconscious desire to reject her womanhood. I seem to have the reverse effect of longing for fulfilled womanhood so much that my curvy figure is my way of embracing myself and of feeling less isolated. By leaving home so young to live abroad I was forced to grow up, which in turn may have been detrimental to my dancing career. It seems to me that it is necessary for a ballet dancer to have a certain childlike innocence and obedience. I think my very independent, individual way often intimidates people, even my superiors, and makes it very difficult for me to conform.

I've returned to Stockholm with a heavy heart. There is so little reason to be here other than to collect my wages until June. At least the workshop gives me sense of purpose, but it seems intangible, especially as I've lost two of my dancers. One has left the company and the other is injured and will not be able to dance again this season. So I have to start again with two new dancers.

April 17th 1986

Thomas Igloi died ten years ago today. I have at last recovered the basic faith in life which his sudden death tore away from me. He is especially close to me in my solitude and listening to recordings of his cello playing brings me a sense of peace.

In the past I have privately dedicated performances to his memory, but today I felt washed out and detached. I barely felt involved in the dress rehearsal of *Romeo and Juliet* though gradually a character was forming in my subconscious. I found myself becoming a young Italian woman of some centuries ago. Though I was still young, I was worn down by my life experiences and no longer a fresh beauty. I had been married and my husband had been killed in a street brawl. I was fed up with all the bloodshed that always meant unhappiness for those left behind, and a mess to be cleaned up. Generally, I was cynical about the way of life in Verona and the petty family feuds. The arrival of a wedding procession cheered me a little; perhaps there was hope for the future and they would soon start making babies to replace some of the dead men. I met my younger brother in the market place and tried to dissuade him from getting involved with the harlots who were dirty and always causing trouble. Grief overwhelmed me when there was fighting again in bitter duels disrupting the wedding celebrations. Somehow I, rather than my character, was very moved and upset when Romeo took his revenge on Tybalt for the death of his friend Mercutio. Tears rolled down my cheeks and I seemed to be crying for every sadness imaginable. I felt totally wrecked afterwards, but it didn't matter as I had nothing more to do.

I've taken a new, young company member under my wing and am teaching her some Benesh Dance Notation. All our repertoire is recorded in this notation, though I am one of the few dancers who can read it. I am also teaching her character dance technique from different countries which is needed in the big classical ballets, but she has never been trained in it before. So this is another little project to keep me busy.

April 23rd 1986

Finally I agreed to meet Alex. It was strange to see him again; nothing has changed. We had lunch and walked around the town. I sense that we both still care for each other, but don't know how to handle the situation. I'm glad I decided to forgive him and we can be friends again.

The current political tension between Libya and the USA which also affects Great Britain frightens me. I suppose it's silly, but I'm afraid something dreadful might happen to London before I return home.

April 25th 1986

It was weird to find myself sitting next to my former director here, Gunilla, in the canteen this afternoon. She asked about my future plans and encouraged me to continue with my choreography. She was very sensitive to the fact that I am so homesick admitting that she would not want to live abroad. She told me that her husband, who is from Yugoslavia, still doesn't really feel at home here after twenty years and being married to a

Swede. Her suggestion I might return as a guest teacher struck me as somehow comical and very unlikely, though I appreciate her confidence in me.

April 26th 1986

At a rehearsal of *Untitled* today I initiated a new dancer into the piece. This time I taught the movements by demonstrating them so she copied, whereas with the other dancer a few days ago I talked more about the source and motivation of the movements and demonstrated much less. I suppose I am experimenting with ways of teaching my choreography. I am probably learning more from the dancers than they are learning from me. There is no specific way to make dances. Each choreographer is different, and I am aware of how I am developing my personal approach by trying out various methods. Inevitably these ways will be constantly changing and renewing themselves as life does and one collaborates with different people. It really is quite fascinating.

April 27th 1986

Yesterday evening was like a cleansing of the soul. It was a way to go away, without going away. It was a party I shall never forget. The most surprising part was my sense of spontaneity and lack of inhibition without losing control.

When I arrived at my Icelandic friends' flat, the party was in full swing and songs resounded. Most people were a little tipsy and a couple of chaps were already on the way down, wandering from room to room, lost souls trying to capture attention to reassure themselves that they were not lonely people behind the drunken facades.

I suppose the jovial chanting from the sitting room intimidated me as I chose to spend most of the evening with the quieter more intellectual types in the kitchen. Most of them spoke good English and I had little opportunity to sit back and enjoy the musical sounds of the Icelandic language punctuated by descriptive gestures.

An apparently crazy character approached me quite early expressing a desire to practise his English. His way was to play the fool making jokes and creating dramatic effects. On the surface he was entertaining, but beyond the mask was a sensitive young man. I spoke with many different people, including a film director who gave me some insights into theatre and film production. He seemed a bit depressed, and my friends told me afterwards that, even after living in Sweden for twenty years, he still misses Iceland and feels he is a foreigner here. He flirted with me intensely, but I played it cool. Later I wondered if I should have taken advantage.

At a certain moment dancing started and I found myself whirled into the centre of it all. I was on my feet dance after dance with different partners. It was nice to feel free and uninhibited without the aid of alcohol. I had been instructed to bring a bottle of whatever I wanted to drink and turned up with a can of tomato juice, much to horror of some seasoned drinkers. Later I was serenaded by a guitar and two men singing Icelandic ballads. Gradually people left and my friends and I, and the crazy chap remained.

My girlfriend and I found ourselves dancing to a waltz, and then the men (who are not dancers) gave a stunning improvisation to the beginning of Stravinsky's *Rite of Spring*. I was prompted into a limited rendering of my silent solo when the question was raised if it is possible to dance without music. Despite being handicapped by lack of space, the wrong clothing and dizziness from lack of sleep (it was about 4am), I procured approval from my audience.

After this I decided it was time to go home, even though I was reluctant to break the atmosphere. No-one else wanted it to end either and an hour later we were all sitting in the kitchen eating breakfast listening to the dawn chorus. Time slipped by and we decided to round off the party by going for a walk in the deserted streets, finishing with coffee at the central station; the only place which is open at 7am on a Sunday. We had to admit defeat after this and I was in bed by 8am.

May 1st 1986

When I showed the women in my dressing room the skirt I am making for my silent solo they immediately suggested I wear it as I showed it to them; topless. Their spontaneous reaction was partly in jest, but when I told them of my intention to be topless, they agreed it was acceptable and beautiful. It gives the solo a new perspective. In no way must the nudity be vulgar, but presented with sincerity it could suggest a mysterious vulnerability. In turn, the skirt gains in importance, especially in the way in which I use it. It appears to represent something symbolic. If the nakedness is the raw emotion, perhaps the skirt is the conscience. I plan to paint all the exposed flesh white, including the legs, to give a ghostly effect. Thus my body will become a little intangible, like a sculpture. The textures of the skirt and the flesh will contrast. I want the face to be white and plastic, and with a simple makeup emphasising only the eyes. I'm not sure about the head. I thought a contrasting black wig, or even loose hair, but perhaps I'll settle for a French roll which suits me and shows my neck line. The creative buzz is surfacing and filling my soul.

The performances are in sight now and I think my patience will pay off with the time I've had to experiment and allow ideas to brew. The result will be all the richer and I'm curious to see what I shall produce. I am giving myself a challenge, especially being the performer, which is most stimulating. The price I pay, as usual, is pain and fatigue. But with retirement so close, it is worth it.

May 4th 1986

Another boring Sunday...

Sunday is the most difficult day to get through when one is alone, and especially when one is physically and emotionally drained. I know I can experience loneliness anywhere, anytime, but I refuse to believe that the emotional torture to which I've been subjected in Stockholm is necessary at such frequent intensity.

I took myself to see an old film of the Bolshoi Ballet. It was dated, but interesting nonetheless. I met a couple of dancers there and suggested we go somewhere for a cup of tea together afterwards. One wanted to clean her windows, and other had to go home and cook for her family. She did not seem happy at the prospect so I told her to be thankful that she had a family to go home to, but she didn't understand what I meant. Thank goodness I only have five more Sundays left in Stockholm.

May 11th 1986

This climate is too much for me! It can be snowing one day, then you close your eyes and when you open them it is summer. Stockholm has burst into a green symphony of foliage in just one week. I feel cheated of the pleasure of watching the transformation and savouring the anticipation of summer. It's just there - slap-bang! I wonder if nuclear waste from the explosion in Chernobyl has influenced nature in some way.

Another dreary Sunday was cheered when Alex took me out for a drink this evening. There is still a lot of unspoken warmth between us.

May 13th 1986

I saw a rainbow this evening. The last time I saw one was in Helsinki. Will this one bring me good fortune with my choreographic endeavours like the last one did?

The final performance of *Nutcracker* has left me drained but relieved I shall never have to dance that fiendish Waltz of the Flowers again.

May 16th 1986

In an extraordinary explosion of creative energy I completed the solo today and made two more minutes of *Untitled*, which is now twelve minutes long. *Solo*, as I've decided to call my silent solo, seems to reflect the contrasts between peace and violence in the world. The opening represents struggle; perhaps reaching to free oneself from one's conscience (the skirt), or stretching to the stars to achieve a dream, or longing to escape from something? At the end I break into an aggressive run which finishes in a position reaching upwards again. After a pause where it looks like the piece is finished, the final movement is of trembling hands lowering to cover my ears. Perhaps the world refuses to hear or recognise the destruction rampant in it. Covering my ears when there is no sound must have some obscure meaning.

I'm impatient for it all to be over so I can start my new life in England. At the same time the work in the studio on my choreography is magically satisfying. The lows are hard and lonely, but the highs are heavenly. I shall probably be sad to leave in many ways.

May 19th 1986

I received a letter from the Estonian chap I met a year ago. It had been posted in Sweden by a friend of his who had visited Estonia. He thought I might not be receiving his letters as he had not heard from me for some time. Indeed, after the first few letters I gave up writing when I ceased to receive replies. I presumed he had forgotten about me or lost interest in the contact. It restores some faith in the human race to discover I was wrong.

May 23rd 1986

The Cancan in *Orpheus in the Underworld* was encored tonight. It's a popular production and I like to be involved in one of its highlights. This compensates for the boredom of waiting for entrances, and the frustration at the banal choreography.

Earlier today *Untitled* and *Solo* were videoed in their completed forms in the studio. If anyone falls out, or the performance is cancelled, I have my "babies" on tape and this gives me a sense of security. *Untitled* is about seventeen minutes long, and *Solo* about seven. The latter was met with applause from my colleagues who were watching it for the first time. I hope no-one complains about my pieces being too short this time as some did before.

May 24th 1986

The last *Sleeping Beauty* brought my farewell to classical ballet performances. I wore glitter on my face to celebrate, to the amusement of the dancers, though it could not be seen by the audience. However, I felt no emotion; I was numbed by the soreness in my body, my own choreography being the culprit. I gave a small party afterwards, announced on the invitations as "burn the ballet shoe party", to celebrate the end of inflamed toe joints and blisters. It was very cosy and I was amazed how eleven dancers fitted into my small flat. Around 2am people decided to leave and we went out in the rain to set light to a pointe shoe in a sort of ritual.

May 30th 1986

I've survived surprisingly well on two hours sleep. It is called "love"... or "passion"... or something like that ...

I met Alex for dinner last night. We ate in an intimate restaurant in the old town and he ordered a bottle of champagne to celebrate the completion of my choreography. In a festive mood we went to our favourite jazz club. Dancing to the live music our bodies gradually moved closer together. He suggested we go to his place. Passion raged through the night and we clung to each other as if for the last time. Nothing was said about meeting again, though Alex did mention his thoughts about trying to work in England for a while.

June 1st 1986

The company spring party is always the highlight of the year, but this time it was the highlight of my three years with the Royal Swedish Ballet. As usual the fancy dress was optional, and this year I decided to dress up. I went as an Arabian princess exposing my midriff to the approval of my male colleagues. Also, as usual, the cabaret had everyone in stitches with laughter, and the dancing was fun. The party spread all over the theatre including climbing up onto the roof where there is a magnificent panoramic view over the city. I'd never ventured up here before. One could see quite far in the half light of a summer's night with the reflected lights sparkling on the Baltic Sea.

Around 3am all but a small group remained and I joined them to watch the sun rise on a nearby island. We took left over food and wine with us and ate a picnic by a fire which we lit. A few hours later, with the sun shining in a clear blue sky, I walked home through the deserted streets with another dancer. It felt as if the city belonged to us.

June 3rd 1986

We are rehearsing in the Marionetten Theatre close to the Opera House. The stage is very small and an awkward shape. Some of the audience cannot see part of it, so movement is restricted to within the part which is in sight of all the seats. However, there is a special intimate feeling which I like.

Untitled is causing me a few problems in communicating the requirements of the dynamics of the movements to the dancers. They are at the stage of knowing the steps and doing them, but now I need to push for more quality and commitment from them. At least the simple costumes are sorted now and I have decided on my lighting.

I had been missing Alex over the weekend and emotions were bubbling up inside me. I confided in my close girlfriend who patiently listened to me and then suggested I call him and talk to him. I told her I felt nervous as if I were going to audition for a job. She calmed me down: "say you don't need a contract, just a few performances!" After all, the relationship is worthy of honesty and communication. Alex invited me over, he had been phoning me all day apparently, but I'd been out.

When I met Alex I was unable to express my confused feelings but summed them up with "I care about you". He started to glow and assured me that he cares about me too. We went out for a drink and then spent the night together.

The romance with Alex is a welcome, possibly essential, distraction from my tension for the workshop. I'm particularly nervous about the costume for *Solo*. I'm sure I would not do this if I were not leaving! With my girlfriend's help I am making the transition from creator to interpreter, which was difficult for me in the beginning. I am finding the tension and sense of struggle which is inherent in it.

June 12th 1986

My spasmodic encounters with Alex are a diamond of escapism amidst the turmoil of pre-premiere nerves, combined with an indefinable emotional reaction to my imminent departure from Sweden.

I sabotaged my last performance at the Opera House in *Orpheus in the Underworld* as much as I dared. They were mostly little things to catch my partners off their guard such as: arriving at the last minute for an entrance, putting a rose in my wig, and wearing my dress off my shoulders. I caused a sensation by painting my face with the design of the Union Jack for the Cancan. The singers said I should do it like that every time; but there won't be another time.

I am getting into the drama of *Solo* more and more, and my fantasy expands each time I do it. At the lighting rehearsal today my friend, who is doing the lighting cues for me, admitted to being so spellbound by the end that she almost forgot to give the fade out cue. A (non-dancer) friend of a dancer in the show who was watching, told me she was moved by my piece too. There is nothing more satisfying to me in the whole world than to know that I have communicated with another soul through my Art.

June 13th 1986

The dress rehearsal is over. Now there are just the three performances left. I'm very happy to have a video from this morning and it was interesting to watch the atmosphere that I create in the solo. My way of moving has matured enormously since I've been here. I was terrified before I went out onstage knowing that most of my colleagues would be there to see my bare torso. One of my choreographer friends told me that she had been initially very shocked by my nudity, but that it fitted with the piece which she had liked very much. She thinks I am very courageous. I agree. I was terrified before I went out onto the stage but my fear was essential to give the solo its strength. Also, I think the element of shocking the audience with the costume is good, because it immediately forces an internal reaction in the viewers which prompts their interest and concentration.

The working atmosphere of our workshop is very special. Everyone is mucking in, putting in energy to support each other and get the show on the road. It's one of life's beautiful experiences.

June 14th 1986

What a buzz! And how wonderful to hear so many positive compliments, even cheers of "Bravo!" as I took my calls. One person told me he thought of Joan of Arc when watching it. Receiving praise from Birgit Culberg, such a renowned choreographer herself, was very satisfying. One of our (slightly crazy) company pianists assured me that I am the crack in the universe!

It was heavy going with two shows today, and I'm thankful to have tomorrow to give my body a chance to recover when I visit Mia's family's summer house on one of the archipelago islands.

After the final performance on Monday I shall be retired! Actually, I'm finding something new in myself through these performances and I'm not sure if this is really the end, or the beginning of something else. I feel inspired to make more solos when I go home. If I can still touch people, and it means so much to me to do this, then I really have no choice in the matter. This isn't to say I should abandon my teaching aspirations, it's just worth being open to the possibilities of performing my choreography.

June 19th 1986
This is a strange time. I am in a sort of burned out trance. The performance on Monday was quite traumatic. I was incredibly nervous and danced as if my life depended on it. I again received a stream of compliments and rapturous applause.

A group of dancers went out to a local pizzeria afterwards and Alex and Mia, who had been in the audience, joined us. I returned with Alex to his flat where he expressed his appreciation of my dancing in a loving way. Another night with little sleep ...

Excitement continued the following morning when the newspaper which was dropped through Alex's letterbox contained an extremely complimentary review of *Solo*. In another newspaper I was compared to Isadora Duncan in my daring to expose my torso. (*Svenska Dagbladet* 19/06/1986)

It's extraordinary to have my greatest success in Stockholm and be seven kilos overweight by previous standards. Anyway, the important thing is that I've been able to turn the turmoil of my recent emotions into something which I can give away to an audience. Knowing that my choreography is so appreciated fills my soul with warmth.

Egon was very complimentary and approved of the way I had followed through my ideas, which is the most constructive comment I've received. It was particularly welcome after his previous criticisms that I could push more. A few people have commented that *Untitled* is too long. I am pleased about this. I agree with them, but I had to drive myself to this extreme after only making short pieces before of five minutes or less. Nonetheless, I found it fascinating to watch from the wings as the dancers developed through the work and I discovered new things about myself every time I saw it. Perhaps the newspaper which mistakenly advertised *Untitled* as "Unlimited" had a point!

June 20th 1986
It took two young men just under an hour and a half to pack all my belongings into boxes and into a removal van. It gave me a peculiar feeling. I felt out of control of the situation and disassociated from even my most treasured possessions. When everything had gone I felt relieved. I almost don't care if my things never arrive in London. The important thing is that I am going home.

I have not been given a grant for the teaching course by Sweden because I am not Swedish, and England will not give me one because I have been living away from the country too long. I am going to find a room to rent near the Royal Academy of Dance so I can be independent from my parents. I'm not too sure how I am going to fund all this once my savings run out. But I've survived the challenges of a ballet career for ten years in four different countries, so I shall survive the challenges ahead.

The last days were spent saying goodbyes. There was a little sadness in this as I shall leave some special friends behind, even though I'm happy to be embarking on a new adventure and going home.

Alex will be leaving Sweden in a couple of months to go on a long travelling holiday. He has vague plans to go to London and perhaps work there. Our parting was not much different from any other. I said something like, "have a nice holiday gypsy", to which he replied, "see you sometime".

Sure! Sometime …

Afterword

After completing the teaching course, I turned down a couple of offers to work abroad again as a teacher, determined to stay in London. During the first year following the course, whilst I established myself on home territory as a freelance teacher and choreographer, I put together this book. My new typing skills were put to use as I collated the text from my diaries and letters. I sent my manuscript off to numerous publishers, but whilst some acknowledged my story had interest, I was an unknown name and it would be hard for them to make good money from it. So the manuscript sat in a cupboard for over thirty years whilst I got on with my life.

If I had had children I would have mentioned to them that the manuscript of my dancing career sat gathering dust in a cupboard, and perhaps one day it would amuse them to read it. As fate would have it, despite finding myself married to an Englishman within four years of leaving Sweden, and my best efforts (another story for another time), I did not succeed in having children.

Thirty-two years after this book ends, both my parents have passed away, and I am happily settled in my second marriage. My father passed away in 2003 aged seventy-eight, so he was not dying in the 1980s as I thought he was. Sadly, he lived the last twenty-eight years of his life battling with constant pain. My mother lived to the grand age of ninety, taking her last breath in January 2018. They were happier when I was back in London, and I was able to be supportive to them both into their old age.

Life now presents me with the opportunity to make choices about how I spend my time after forty-two years of earning a living as a dance professional.

One of the choices I make is to revisit this manuscript, retype the whole book in electronic form, and review it. I have re-read the diaries as I do this and made small amendments. I feel it is a huge egocentric self indulgence to present this book for publication. Is my story really that interesting? Who knows. But if one person thinks it is, then it will have been a worthwhile indulgence.

Whilst reworking this book, I have reflected on how life has changed, how different my experience would be over thirty years later. If I were a dancer now in 2019, I would be able to have constant contact with friends and family through the internet. The loneliness would be so much easier to bear if I could call home on Skype or FaceTime. I would spend hours of my free time watching my favourite dancers on YouTube, probably instead of the hours of self therapy writing in my diary. With cheap flights it would be easy to pop home more often and for friends to visit me, especially in Sweden which was very expensive to fly to thirty years ago.

Perhaps it will be sobering for dancers today to realise how much times have changed, and although dance remains a gruelling and challenging profession, there is a lot of support available if a dancer is sensible enough to look for it. Above all I would urge any dancers reading this and recognising themselves in the weight obsessive mindset, to take a moment to remember that the body is the dancer's instrument and it deserves respect and good maintenance. Preoccupation with body image may well still be at the forefront of a dancer's mind, but malnourishment is not a way to treat that body. In today's society there are nutritionists available to help dancers to fuel their bodies appropriately. Please seek that help if you need it.

The knowledge I now have about the harm I did to my body with my erratic eating habits, being under weight and not having periods, would not have changed my choices. A sensible nutritionist might have helped, and with emotional support I believe the eating habits might have been less destructive. Today I would still need to be skinny in order to hope to have a job as a ballet dancer, because my shape just isn't right. So I still would have experienced times of amenorrhea (loss of periods) and probably, I would have experienced low bone density and osteoporosis. Nothing could change the shape of my skeleton and "physical limitations". Under the circumstances, in retrospect, I think I did the best I could with what I had. I no longer chide myself for what I did not achieve, but applaud myself for what I did accomplish.

Mental health is so much better understood now, and I would be able to have counselling. Some of the large ballet companies nowadays have in-house therapists. I needed this sort of support, but was terrified of asking for it in case my medical records would then show that I was mentally unstable, and that this would be held against me in some way. I thought that caring about my weight and being homesick, made me mentally unstable.

Would I chose to be a dancer again, knowing what I now know? Probably yes, because I never felt it was a choice; I felt it was a calling.

Was it worth it? Yes, I don't regret any of it, and feel blessed for the rich experiences I had.

Was life easier when I stopped being a dancer and became a teacher and choreographer? Oh yes! I still performed my own choreography and produced two one woman shows. I was not skinny, and the audience did not complain! Teaching opened a whole new world of opportunities to share my passion for dance.

Did I feel at peace and rooted to be back in London? I certainly did.

Was it as wonderful as I dreamed to be in a loving, stable relationship and not be lonely all the time? Yes, and yes.

Appendix i

September 1986

On *Untitled* and *Solo*

I worked for a long time with ideas, building the form as I went along with no clear idea of where I was going - just a blurred image. I enjoy creating spontaneously, not being tied down to a musical score or story. When I work this way my choreography becomes very close to my personal progression in life and reflects my soul very intimately, for those who are sensitive enough to appreciate this. Basically, I did what I set out to do, which would have satisfied me regardless of critic's or colleague's opinions. In fact, I achieved more.

The most difficult thing about success, is following it. One is so afraid to fail, or cease to progress. Thus it gave me enormous satisfaction to realise that with my *Solo* I'd created a piece just as strong and original, if not more so, as *Birdsong*. My triumph gave me hope that having achieved one success and progressed to another, I might be able to continue to work and dig into the roots of my soul for something worthwhile and beautiful to say to the world.

Untitled was different. It was less appreciated than the solo though it did have some admirers. The point of this piece was an exercise for myself in choreography, rather than the creation of a masterpiece. Previous pieces of mine have been criticised for being too short. This was the only fault people found. That some people considered *Untitled* to be too long, was, I thought, a victory. There was a misprint in one of the newspapers announcing it as "Unlimited". I thought this was hilariously funny as it quite suits the piece as a title. Naming it *Untitled* was meant to be a way of challenging the audience's imagination. It was a wonderful experience to work on it. I learned so much from my dancers; much more than they realise. It was also fascinating to watch the performances. The dancers improved all the time, and I constantly caught reflections of myself in their movements and presentation. It was uncanny; like a child which strongly resembles a parent.

To most people *Untitled* took the form of a prolonged abstract dance with interesting and pleasing moments, which is what I set out to do. However, I am not able to produce movements without them automatically having life born of ideas and emotions. So in order to keep the piece contained within a framework of design, I arranged my ideas in a progressive form.

Originally it was going to be a solo and I decided to base it on London and put my constant homesickness to some positive use. So I bought some records of sound effects of London and listened to them. I decided Big Ben would make a good opening; something strong to wake up the audience and get their attention. This is heard in darkness. Then on the twelve strokes of the clock, a diagonal tunnel of light appears on the stage with a dancer moving through it in time with the chimes.

As I became involved in the choreographic work, I also became more involved with my life in Stockholm and the homesickness eased. So I could no longer draw on that feeling for ideas. Instead, the choreography grew as my experiences broadened and I chose to involve more dancers. At first I wanted six dancers to challenge myself, but for various reasons I was forced to use three, which turned out fine in the end.

Once I'd decided which sounds to use, the form of the piece started to fall into place. After Big Ben, I use an "eerie wind" representing the blowing away of my homesickness and transition into a new life experience. Then, when all three dancers have entered the stage, I introduce sounds from the street: Paternoster Square in London, which sounds appropriately busy. All the sound effects are linked by passages of silence.

I evolved a vocabulary of original movements and built on phrases with variations, so everything is held together in a tight unity of style. Some dancers managed to grasp my ideas quite quickly, others took longer to get their bodies to respond the way I wanted. I use rather static statuesque poses in my movement line. This is punctuated by soft bouncing movements between two limbs of a dancer, or limbs of two dancers. Each dancer moves individually and seldom consciously in unison. The idea of everyone repeating similar steps but in different positions on the stage and at varying speeds, is that we all share similar experiences in life, but they feel different to us because we might be in a different circumstance. Then every so often we meet someone and that meeting influences us both in some way. Thus, the bodies of two dancers meet and then rebound causing them to move in a new direction.

At this point I had the three dancers moving in various patterns at varying speeds, occasionally meeting, but never communicating; my cynical observation of life. How was I going to resolve this?

I couldn't see a reasonable conclusion other than to use a circle (in a clockwise direction) symbolising that, though we may feel very isolated in our personal struggles, we are all part of the same universe and are all involved in the same endless struggle with life. Hence, the dancers move into a circle formation repeating the same sequence of movements. This is performed at different speeds at first, until gradually they move in harmonious unison. The unison is very difficult for the dancers to execute perfectly as they can not always see each other depending on the part of the sequence which they are performing, and there are no musical cues. Their effort creates an interesting tension between the dancers. For the final sound, I chose the sea - the eternal sea.

I certainly followed my idea through and I have the foundations of an interesting piece. I think it was not seen to advantage because we had a very awkward performance space to work in. I was not strong and positive enough about my requirements of the dancers early enough in the process; the ideas formed very slowly. Nor did I have enough rehearsal time to work with the final cast of dancers, remembering that I lost dancers through injury and leaving the company. It wasn't bad in the end, it was quite acceptable, but it could have been better.

Costumes were a problem. I wanted something simple, but not looking like class uniform. In the end I dug out a couple of tops I had knitted some time ago for the two girls. They were loosely knitted resembling chain armour. One girl wore tights, the other made her own pair of shorts which suited her well. One day I noticed the boy wearing an attractive peach t-shirt and asked him to put it away and wear it for the performances with brown tights. The colour scheme was gold, peach, rust and brown; my favourite earthy colours.

Solo starts with the dancer standing feet slightly apart, arms reaching diagonally upwards in a V shape. The focus is upwards representing Robert Browning's famous quotation "Ah! But a man's reach must exceed his grasp, or what's a heaven for?" She is lit by a single circle of downlight. Not flattering, but giving a message of enclosure.

The movements are structured in a similar way to *Birdsong* using contrasting ideas in the form: moving and static, quick and slowly controlled. The movements contrast between contraction and extension.

It starts calmly with the tension contained in the body. Then an energy builds up to a sort of frenzy, like life goes out of control from time to time, and the circle of light expands. In the original version of *Silent Song*, which uses the same opening as *Solo*, the boy entered at this point. His presence calmed the scene developing into a rather victorious conclusion where he lifted the girl closer to heaven. Whereas in the new version, the frenzy causes me, the dancer, to fall to the floor and then become frozen in a pose of fear. I resolve this by using the long skirt as a symbol of protection or shelter. Now I have a key for the continuation.

I hadn't used the skirt at all in the earlier concept. Now it became an all important symbol. Using the skirt, the dance progresses in a circle along the border of the circle of light. Thus, with the comforting support of the skirt, it is possible to move to the extremity of the light. The circle of light could represent the world, the unknown, whatever you want. As the pace accelerates the skirt slips from my grip. Then I return to the original pose reaching upwards, but this time facing the back and holding the skirt again. In other words, I have the strength to go on reaching if my back is turned from the audience, and I have the symbolic support of the skirt. However, I didn't like this ending. I didn't like what it told me about myself needing an emotional crutch. Choreography can really expose the creator's soul. I was frustrated. I felt trapped and I longed to break out. From my very intense emotions came the next section where, in an explosion of physical energy, a sequence of movements just poured out of me.

Sometimes I decide that I'm going to go into the studio and work, and I have coax and push my body into moving. Sometimes my body tells me it must work in a turmoil of physical energy and emotion so strong, that I fear I shall become violent if I don't. So I do. Now I use the skirt briefly in a more aggressive way and it becomes a weapon in my battle. Resolving this rather intense piece of warfare took a long time. Ideas seemed constipated. Eventually, I discovered a door to a new phase, and was gratified to explore a moment of glory. I nicknamed this section: the angels. More constipation followed. I knew the choreography was very strong up until this point. How was I going to find a worthy ending?

I had several weeks left before the workshop performances, so I just stopped and put it on a shelf; so to speak. It was during this period that the idea for the costume came to me in a burst of inspiration. I had bought material and made a beautiful creamy white, full circle, waist to ankle skirt, as soon as I'd decided to perform the solo in the workshop. As I worked with the skirt and it took on a symbolic importance, it became increasingly difficult to decide what to wear from the waist up. The skirt was so strong that the upper body had to maintain a balance of strength in the presentation. I played with various ideas of cuts of leotards, but everything broke the line. Visually the impression was very clear to me: one thing was being said below the waist line, and another above it. I decided to go for the natural simplicity of nudity: two textures in contrast, flesh and material. In order to be sure that there were no misunderstandings or sexual implications, I painted my entire body and face white. I wore pants under the skirt which were carefully concealed by the choreography.

I'd never imagined myself experiencing any kind of nudity onstage, mostly because I was embarrassed about my imperfect classical shape. But with my feminine hips concealed under the skirt I decided, as the choreographer, that my beautiful torso could be exposed. As the performer, I was petrified. I certainly would never have dared to do this unless I was about to leave the country! My very real fear gave my performance an intended tension and commitment. My bare torso served as an element of shock for the audience, guaranteeing their attention and opening the doors for communication.

Then Chernobyl happened; the nuclear explosion in Russia. The fallout of radiation was rather too close to Sweden for comfort. I had been very disturbed by both the assassination of Olof Palme (the Swedish prime minister) earlier in the year, and the American attack on Libya using British bases, just ten days before the Chernobyl accident. It was a strange time; the beginning of May and the sudden blossoming of greenery in the Swedish spring. I was involved in my choreography and constantly "high", as if on a drug, or "low" with withdrawal symptoms. Choreography can do that to you. It's a constant performance, a challenge you live with twenty-four hours a day, even when the job seems done. Choreography is the ultimate love affair! If you are an artist who is driven, it is simultaneously daring, ecstatic and terrifying.

Thus, came the end.

I am standing proudly holding my skirt high with hope. I break into a contraction with sobbing movements and wrap myself in the folds of the skirt; not believing in the hope, begging the skirt to save me again. Then suddenly I start running and throwing the skirt away with violence and anger until I come to a stop holding the skirt forcefully towards the sky with both hands close together. A desperate plea for salvation perhaps? The skirt slips between my fingers to the ground. My eyes follow it in disbelief. Then I reach back up again as if to say: "what does all this mean?" The pose is almost identical to the opening one. It could be the end. Perhaps the audience thinks that it is the end. Then from the extreme tension of my reach upwards, my hands begin to tremble, and with great resistance they move downwards to shield my ears. Simultaneously the circle of light closes around me to become a spotlight, as at the beginning. Then there is blackout.

The seven minutes of *Solo* are in complete silence apart from my occasional heavy breathing and panting.

Appendix ii

All my life I occasionally wrote poems. Here are a couple which I feel strongly relate to this memoir.

A childhood poem:

Love

Love is a throbbing pain,

An aching sore inside.

Love is a sympathetic understanding,

Love is difficult to hide.

Love is an ever burning ambition,

Love is wanting something more.

Love is never being parted,

Love is giving from the core.

A poem written two days after the young cellist I was in love with as a teenager, Thomas Igloi, died. I want to include it in this book as a tribute to such a wonderful and talented young man who was taken from this world far too early.

Pourquoi m'as tu quittée?   *19/04/1976*

Oh mon amour! Pourquoi m'as tu quittée

Quand nous avions toutes nos vies devant nous?

Il y a tant de choses que j'aurais bien voulu te dire,

Maintenant je ne pourrais jamais t'en parler.

Pourquoi as-tu dû mourir

Sans savoir que je t'aime?

Pourquoi as-tu dû mourir?

Toi, qui étais si gai, si gentil, si doué, si sensible,

Toi, qui a été mon premier amour

Toi, qui seras toujours dans mon coeur.

Est-ce possible Dieu

Qu'un si grand artiste

Avec un avenir si certain, si beau,

Pouvait mourir?

Tu ne m'as jamais comprise mon amour,

Car je devais toujours cacher mes sentiments pour toi.

197

Et maintenant

Tu ne sauras jamais.

Oú est ce sourire avec les yeux verts

Ouverts et brillants que ne je verrais plus jamais?

Oú est cette voix riante et mélodieuse

Que je n'entendrai plus jamais?

Oú sont ces fortes mains

Douces et gentilles, que je ne toucherai plus jamais?

Oú est ce corps

Qui ne respire plus?

Il ya tant de questions, mon amour,

Auxquelles je ne pourrai jamais répondre.

Mais il y a une chose que je peux te promettre,

Je tiendrai toujours ta mémoire tendrement dans mon coeur.

Photographs

Aged Four

Aged Fifteen
Photograph by Gerald Howson

Aged Seventeen
Photograph by Gerald Howson

On my balcony in Düsseldorf

Odette in *Swan Lake* - Dublin 1980

Amsterdam 1980

Sculptures

Ariadne - Stockholm 1985

Birdsong - Helsinki 1984
Photograph by Sarah L Lawson

Solo - Stockholm 1986
Photograph by Enar Merkel Rydberg

Acknowledgements

and Copyright

I would like to thank Glenn Altern and Kerry Stirton who read the very first draft back in the 1980s and helped me form the original text. A big thank you to Tracy Field for giving me unprejudiced feedback as someone who knew little about the Ballet world. A special thank you to Rebecca Howson for her proof reading and pertinent observations. My thanks also to Jacqueline Beteinber Zeto for her corrections of my French in the poem "Pourquoi m'as tu quittée". Any errors in the final copy are mine.

Please contact the author for any queries:

ysabelletaylorballet@yahoo.com

First published Independently in 2019.

Made in the USA
Monee, IL
10 November 2022

17445736R00118